"What a remarkable book! Lisa Jones's courageous journey through the loss of her young husband to discovering joy and meaning in her life is deeply compelling and inspirational. It's so well written that there were times when I was so caught up in the story that I wanted to race ahead to see what happened, the same way I do in a paperback thriller. And there were times that I was touched beyond measure at the valiant vulnerability of this story. I highly recommend this book."

— **Denise Linn**, best-selling author of 18 books, including *Sacred Space* and *Soul Coaching*®

"As a filmmaker, I first knew Lisa (Sharpe) Jones as an actress of great spirit and sensitivity. Thus, I could not have been surprised that she would channel this same spirit and sensitivity into her writing. However, her memoir *Art of Living Happy* is a revelation of sorts. Weaving seamlessly between universally shared human dramas of love, death and money and the more inexplicable realm of the Wisdom of the Ages, psychic phenomenon and angels, Lisa invites us to share in her journey to spiritual awakening with such a simple and direct style that believers and disbelievers will all relate in some way to her quest to find her own truth and to live it fully. A captivating and inspiring journey from start to finish."

— **David Giardina**, award-winning filmmaker and director of *Taffy Was Born*

"Lisa Jones intimately engages the reader in the experience of the loss of her beloved husband and the discovery of a new life, and everything in between. With courage and tenacity, and the promise of tomorrow, she gives the reader permission to step through grief, experience love again, explore new avenues of life, and she whole-heartedly encourages the reader to be the champion of their destiny.

"With God, Spirit, Angels and her beloved departed family members by her side, Lisa embarks on a life-altering journey that will envelope you. Her words, stories and experiences will gently remind you that you, too, can weather the storms of life.

"Her greatest lesson is: "Until you are aware of why you believe in certain ideas, you just take them as truth, rather than wondering how you came to them." Truth lives deep within the sanctuary of the heart. *Art of Living Happy* is not just a book, it's an experience of life."

— **Roland M. Comtois**, author of *And Then There Was Heaven, A Journey of Hope and Love*, and *16 Minutes ... When One Breath Ends, Another Begins*

art of LIVING HAPPY

After the Loss of a Loved One:

A Real-Life Awakening

Lisa Jones

LIVING HAPPY
PRODUCTIONS

NEW YORK • SAN FRANCISCO • LONDON

Author's note

This is a work of nonfiction. The events and experiences detailed herein are all true, and have been faithfully rendered as the author has remembered them to the best of her ability. Some names, identities and circumstances have been changed to protect the privacy and/or anonymity of the various individuals involved.

DEDICATION

To Spirit

You pushed, and I flew. Now others fly with me.

PROLOGUE

Something Out of Nothing

March 21, 2012
The Ridgefield Playhouse, Ridgefield, CT

I felt the pounding force of all eyes on me at center stage. I sat in the director's chair and tried to focus on what I was there to do. To my right were three stools of different heights nestled closely together, all covered by a green tablecloth—making it faintly resemble a lopsided table. A dusty silk flower arrangement filled with sunflowers, red roses and greenery sat on one of the stools. I had my "Calling All Angels" essential-oil spray and my three favorite crystals placed on one of the other stools. Behind me was a screen awash with a lavender glow. The spotlight was directly over me, both harsh and comforting.

With my eyes closed, I opened my arms and lifted them. Then I spoke:

"I call on God, Universe, Source Energy. I call upon Archangel Michael to stand behind me. I call on Archangel Raphael to stand to my right, Archangel Gabrielle to stand to my left, and in front of me, I call upon Archangel Metatron. Please allow me to be a clear and concise channel for the highest and greatest good for all involved."

Though this was my first time doing this on a stage, I was familiar with what to expect. At this point, I would typically begin to feel tingles or an energetic change at the top of my head, also known as the crown chakra. I would feel my head bob forward and back ever so slightly. These were signs that channeling had begun. This time, to my absolute horror, nothing was happening. In fact, I was getting worse than nothing; sweat was prickling my underarms and my heart had sped up—I thought it would burst out of my chest.

I kept my eyes closed and screamed inside my head for my angels to come and save me. This was supposed to be my big moment and I was left hanging, stuck in front of 140 people who had paid to come to see me channel for them. And they were staring at me getting nothing. *Absolutely nothing.* I was dying out there, wishing I could disappear. I wondered if I would have to give everyone's money back. I thought I'd have to do something else with my life. I was just about to go into a full-blown panic when something inside me took over. Rather than running, I did the opposite of what my fear and insecurity was telling me to do. I walked right up into the moment and faced it.

CHAPTER 1

Eight Years Earlier
February 22, 2004

Just before 6 a.m., I rolled over and snuggled up to Ian. As I draped my arm across his chest and shifted my legs closer to his body, I felt something cold and wet. My eyes flew open as if I had heard an alarm. Ian had never had an incontinence problem, and I never dreamed that he ever would, but there he was, completely oblivious, lying in a pool of his own urine.

I gently shook his shoulder. "Sweetie, wake up."

He turned his head toward my voice and slowly opened his eyes. "I'm thirsty."

"Honey, we need to clean you up. You peed in the bed!" My adrenaline was pumping as I calculated how best to handle this.

He didn't want to get out of bed, so I got up and helped him roll to his right side, and I pulled the soiled sheets out from under him. Then I rolled him to his left and took the linens off the bed. I stretched a clean towel underneath him for the time being.

This is what had become of things.

When Ian first went to the doctor for a swollen lymph node seven years prior, I had no way of knowing that an epic battle with cancer would ensue, just as I couldn't know his cancer, and his death, would change my life.

The previous morning, Ian had awakened incoherent. Throughout his illness, I'd never seen him lose himself, and now he was suddenly becoming a stranger to me. I was terrified at turning this new corner, but being a mother, I was mostly worried how it would affect the children.

The kids were up around 9 a.m. that morning, bickering from the start. They obviously knew something was up. Overwhelmed with having to explain the current situation to them on my own, I called my therapist and asked for advice. It was something I was doing more and more in those final days with Ian. She suggested that I prepare them and explain, "Daddy might not make sense."

I called for the kids to come to Robbie's room. When all three of us were there, I teared up. "I don't want to scare you, but Daddy is starting to say things that don't make sense. His brain is starting to slow down and..."

Jenna, a stoic ten year old at the time, asked outright, "Is Daddy going to die?" Her scared eyes began widening. She usually kept things inside, but I could tell that this was going to be tough for her to bottle up.

"Yes," I said.

Eight-year-old Robbie started screaming, "No! No! No! I don't want my Daddy to die!"

Jenna turned and ran out of the room. Robbie kept screaming. "Why can't we get a doctor? Call a doctor!"

I tried to calm him. "Sweetie, come here. There's nothing more the doctors can do. Come here."

"No! Why did we come home? We should have stayed in Seattle."

My heart broke for my son, who was too young to

have to go through anything like this. I pulled him tightly to me, cradling him in my arms as I used to do; we both sobbed. "I'm so sorry, baby. I'm so sorry. There's nothing more the doctors could do for us in Seattle. They did everything they could. Daddy needs to go to heaven. It's almost time for him to go."

After some time passed, something changed in Robbie. My son finally relaxed in my arms. "Can I go...can I go see Daddy?"

"Yes, sweetie. Let's go see Daddy."

We walked down the hallway hand in hand. Robbie let go and started running. He jumped onto the bed and gave Ian a huge hug.

I was relieved to see Jenna was already in there cuddling with her dad. Usually she ran from scary situations, but this time she had run *to* her father, who was withering away right in front of us. Ian seemed lucid in that moment. He slowly turned and gave Robbie a hug back; he whispered to him how he loved him, promising he would always be with him. He then calmly spoke to Robbie and Jenna about how he was feeling. These final moments Ian had with our children brought me enormous relief. In fact, it brought a sense of peace to the whole ordeal.

Initially, I was mad at myself for not telling the kids earlier about their dad's prognosis. We had been told three days earlier that the cancer was continuing to spread, but I realized that Ian and I hadn't been ready. We were still processing it ourselves.

Telling the kids worked out better than I could have hoped. Once it was out there, the kids responded so maturely and lovingly. They seemed to be processing and accepting it. Robbie and I went downstairs and watched some TV, while Jenna stayed and snuggled with Ian for awhile. When she came downstairs, she said that he wasn't making any sense; rather than it panicking her, she was glad that I had warned her about it.

No one ever had taught me how to handle things like this, so I was forced to make my way in the dark. I did the best I could—I had to guide two young children through the ordeal of watching their dad die in front of them, while simultaneously losing the dream of what my life would be.

Later, Ian suggested that we watch the movie *Grease* as a family. Ian had somehow moved his body to the middle of the bed. He had hardly moved since Thursday evening, when he had come upstairs for the last time. Robbie and Jenna sat on either side of Ian, and I turned on the DVD. The normalcy was wonderful, just sitting as a family and watching a movie. About twenty minutes into it, Ian had to get up and use the bathroom. I knew it would be a process, so I asked the kids to go play downstairs.

He was barely able to stand, teetering his way towards the bathroom, me spotting him along the way. I helped him to walk through the vanity area and around the partition into the open part of the bathroom. We stopped in front of the door to the toilet. He slid his underwear to the floor and painstakingly stepped out of them.

"I don't need your help," he said, stretching his shaking arm out to the doorframe.

He shuffled into the small room with the toilet. It took him a few minutes to maneuver his body into a position so he could sit down. I stood helplessly next to the double sinks watching him. He abruptly closed the door.

As I turned, my eyes landed in the bathroom mirror. I stared so hard that I crawled inside of it. I burrowed deep into the blue hollows of my eyes. I stared and stared back. I didn't recognize myself, and yet I knew who I was and what I had to do—I just didn't want to do it anymore. Part of me wanted to run and never come back, but I knew that I was in this for the long haul. *Till death do us part.*

After several seconds, which felt like an eternity, I went back into the bedroom to put fresh sheets on the bed.

14

LISA JONES

Five minutes passed. "What's the next step? Lisa? Come in here!" Ian impatiently called out from behind the closed door.

"What?" I walked back to the bathroom and opened the door. Ian was sitting on the toilet.

"What's the next step?"

Haltingly, I said, "Did you wipe?"

He was slumped forward, his head looking down, his forearms resting heavily on his weakened thighs.

"No. I mean what treatment options are available?" His body was trembling.

When I had called the doctor to report Ian's disorientation the day before, he told me we were very near the end; it was time to call hospice. I was feeling burdened by this information, but Ian had told me that he didn't want to know until he specifically *asked* to hear it. Now he was ready, and I was honestly relieved not to have to carry it alone anymore. It was simply too heavy.

"Honey, the doctor told me..." I hesitated, gathering up how to tell him. "He told me that he had reviewed your CAT scan, and it didn't look good. He feels there are no other options that could help you at this point."

Silence.

"Sweetie..." I put my hand on his back. "How do you...?"

"I figured that was the case," he said, resigned to his reality.

Not knowing what to do, I could only stand there. Ian zoned out and started muttering to himself.

I waited a minute or so and then interrupted. "Do you want to take a shower and get cleaned up?"

He agreed.

"Okay, come on. Stand up. Good. Let's get you in the shower. I think you'll feel better."

I never thought I would have to bathe my husband. It was the first time during all of his illness that he needed

15

this type of help from me. Although we had been married for almost thirteen years and had been together for fifteen, the thought of having to get into the shower with him and wash his hair, his skin, his private parts, felt overwhelming; it was simply too intimate. Ian was an extremely private person, as was I. We weren't the type of couple that walked around each other naked. Bodily functions were not experienced nor even discussed in front of one another. I felt that he might actually resent me washing his body and find it demeaning. I was not mentally prepared at all for this. Yet, here we were.

I propped Ian by the wall, placed a plastic folding chair into the shower stall, and then changed into shorts and a tank top. I guided him to the shower entrance, assisting him as he stepped over the threshold. He sat in the chair, and I removed his once white T-shirt, which smelled of perspiration, urine and illness. I turned on the water and adjusted the temperature to make it warm. I began to spray his body. I had to be extremely careful not to allow the dangling plastic tube embedded in his chest to get wet.

As I washed his shrunken 125-pound body, something beautiful and lovely rose to the surface. Here was a man returned to a child. He sat innocently, depending on me for this basic act. It's strange how something that I thought was going to be disturbing turned into something wonderful. A robust 230-pound man only a few years earlier, he had now become a small boy once again.

****

When Ian was born, his mother JoAnn didn't want him. She was still married to Ian's father, Bob Sharpe, at the time, but she wanted to leave him to reunite with the man that she had lived with for several years as a common-law wife. She had a five-year-old daughter with this other man. Bob and JoAnn had separated before she gave birth, and the man would not let JoAnn bring the newborn Ian, *someone else's child*, into his home.

Hours after Ian's birth, JoAnn signed adoption papers, releasing her parental rights and turning custody over to the state. His first moments, though he couldn't know it, were soaked in pain and rejection.

Informed by his friend about the birth, Bob stormed the hospital and demanded custody of his child. Given that it was 1959 and that single dads didn't typically rear babies on their own, Bob called upon his sisters to help. They gladly took their nephew in for the first several months of his life.

Soon afterwards, Bob began dating Marian Smith, a secretary at his law firm who was a divorcée with a thirteen-year-old son named Mike. Within a couple of months, Marian and Bob were married. They moved into a new house and brought Ian home.

Marian officially adopted Ian. Bob gave Marian total authority over Ian and his care, with the only caveat being that no one was ever to utter his biological mother's name. However, Marian felt compelled to keep tabs on JoAnn, so that when the day came she could give Ian any and all the information that he desired. Ian was never interested. It was simple to him; if his biological mother didn't want him, he didn't want her either.

When Ian first got sick, I realized I'd never seen a picture of him being baptized, nor had he spoken about it. I prayed that he had, so I asked him about it. He said he didn't know and didn't care. *How could he not care? Wasn't he concerned about his soul? Didn't he realize that there was a chance he would rot in hell?* Even though he attended Jesuit High School in Sacramento, he was one of the few boys there who was not Catholic.

I decided to track down Ian's aunt in California who raised him the first six months of his life. Aunt Dottie didn't remember getting him baptized, but she did give me the name of her church so I could call and check the records myself. I called and found that there was no record there. At this point, I was alarmed.

I grilled Ian's adoptive mother about it. I sat across from her in the pinstriped swivel chair and launched right in: "I was just wondering if you ever had Ian baptized? Maybe you have a record of it. Do you think the hospital baptized him at his birth?"

She raised her eyebrows above her baby blue eyes. Her perfectly coiffed white hair was drawn straight back and delicately secured at the nape of her neck. Her socks coordinated with the hair clip, as was her way. A small uncomfortable laugh escaped from her throat.

"Lisa, you know churches and I don't get along. I can't even walk into one without bursting into tears. Why on earth would I get Ian baptized? Why do you even care?" Her formal manner stiffened more than usual.

Completely desperate now, I let it explode out of me: "Marian, don't you get it? If Ian wasn't baptized, he won't go to heaven!"

She was not fazed; in fact, she seemed dismissive. "Oh, don't be silly dear. Ian is going to be fine, just fine."

She seemed just so sure of herself and what she supposedly knew. In fact, she didn't think he was going to die at all. She was in total denial, just like Ian's stepbrother, Mike, and even Ian himself at the time. Back then, I was the only one that accepted what was going to happen. I just wasn't sure what would happen to Ian *after* he died, and that was what I found so terrifying—it was almost more terrifying than his death itself.

****

As Ian sat on the plastic shower chair, he suddenly became coherent. "I'm ready to know the timeframe. I must know the timeframe in order to assess my supply load."

I wasn't sure, but I thought I understood. He had told the doctor on Wednesday that he couldn't bear to hear how much time he had left but would ask if and when he needed that information. That time seemed to be right now.

I broached it carefully. "The doctor told me that it would probably... be within the week. What do you think about that?"

"That sounds doable. That sounds good."

He seemed resigned to this future, almost calm about it. At that moment, the burden rose off me. Satisfied, Ian immediately went back inside his own head, speaking of nonsensical things.

When I finished showering him, he looked new— shiny and clean, as a baby would. I began to dry his body with one of the towels we had received as a wedding gift years earlier.

"Who are all those people downstairs?" he asked.

"*All those people*? You mean your mom, your brother, and the kids?" Marian, who was having a very difficult time with all this, had reluctantly come over that morning after I explained that Ian was becoming more and more incoherent.

Mike and his wife Betsy had arrived from New Hampshire that morning as well. However, Betsy was back at Marian's as they had brought their two rambunctious cairn terriers, which I didn't want running around the house.

Jenna was getting her things together to sleep over at a friend's house. Robbie was patiently waiting for me to finish our game of, of all things, *Life*. (I was too exhausted to see the poetry in this.) We had started playing earlier in the day, but with all of the distractions we never got a chance to actually finish it. *Life* was put on hold so we could go about the business of life. And death.

"No, there are hundreds of people down there!" he insisted.

I understood what he was saying. "They must all be here for you!" I told him. I had read a book written by hospice workers about how those near death were able to see loved ones on the other side of the veil. Ian was near his end. I led him back to the freshly made bed and got him comfortable with a pair of Depends underwear and his favorite Minnesota Twins T-shirt.

A boxed air mattress lay on the floor. There was also a plastic covered shower chair, a walker and a bedside commode. These items had been delivered from hospice about three hours earlier. I wasn't ready to deal with them, so I had pushed everything into the corner of the room. The oxygen compressor, which had arrived even earlier in the day, made a loud whirring noise.

Just then Jenna ran in to say goodbye. "Bye, Dad. I love you." She bounded up onto the bed and gave Ian the biggest hug her petite body could muster. Her long blond hair flew into the air and spread across her back. Ian's fingers got caught in its web as he hugged her back.

"Let me take a picture of the two of you." I had one of those disposable cameras on the bedside table. "Smile."

Jenna turned her head towards me. Her blue eyes glistened. Ian opened his eyes wide and forced out a giant smile. I've never actually seen that printed photo of the two of them, as I must have lost the camera, but I don't need to; that moment is permanently burned onto my brain.

After Ian was asleep, I went downstairs and called my friend Lisa, whose husband was also battling cancer. She shared with me what to do when a person dies: "You first call the hospice nurse, so they can pronounce the person dead. Then call the funeral director. It's best to call them both at the same time, so that once the nurse is done, the body can be whisked off as soon as possible." I guessed the only way to learn these things was to have them happen to you. An irony of life: You learn everything just at the time you need to know it. Never before.

At about 10 p.m., I went upstairs to get ready for bed and saw that Ian was sleeping peacefully. I turned the water on and let it run to get hot, looking at myself in the mirror. I noticed that the waist of my pants was bunched up where the leather belt had drawn the belt loops close together so my jeans wouldn't fall down. I had lost about fifteen pounds in the three months since we had arrived home to Connecticut. I looked to be on the verge of anorexia. The dark roots were beginning to show through my highlighted blond hair way more than I liked. As I continued to stare into the mirror, I lost myself. I wasn't surprised by what I saw: dark circles under my eyes, gaunt cheeks, acne-covered skin and haunted eyes. I fell into a trance. Was this really my life?

I brushed my teeth, feeling the bristles on my gums and thinking of what was to come. Such routine in such chaos. As I washed my face, the hot water felt like acid, yet it felt good because it at least made me feel something. I went to the closet and pulled on a blue T-shirt and some old soft flannel pajama bottoms. When I turned to walk back into the bedroom, I noticed Ian's bedside lamp was on. The rest of the room was dim. The two windows on either side of the bed were closed, and the curtains were drawn.

Ian shifted in the bed. My eyes were drawn to his face. He looked both serene and ravaged. There was a visible blessing that came with sleep: no pain. His cheeks were sunken, his brown hair a wisp of its former self, his skin sallow and hanging. His mouth had become distorted; his protruding jaw line seemed disproportionate, too big for his small face. It was as though his skull was peering out from beneath his skin. These changes had happened so gradually that I had almost become unaware of them, yet when we went out, I could feel people staring at us.

I caught sight of the new wedding ring on Ian's finger, an extravagant yellow gold and platinum band, one that would really last. I had given it to him a week ago as a surprise Valentine's Day gift. His fingers had shrunk so much over the years of treatments that his old wedding band was swimming on his finger. We were continually looking around the house to see where it had last fallen. He finally had to permanently take it off.

His face showed the stress and strain of the fight. The scar on his neck seemed to grow as his body shrunk. It was the original sight of the lymphoma, a swollen lymph gland that had been removed seven years earlier. It had never healed properly.

I bent over and kissed his forehead, "Goodnight, my love. Sleep well."

I heard the doorbell and knew Ian's best friend Pierre had arrived. When I had called him the day before and told him that the end was near, he booked the next flight to Connecticut. From the stairs, I saw Mike welcoming Pierre at the door and heard their hushed voices buried in their embrace.

Seeing how exhausted I was, Mike and Pierre said they'd take over, and I let them. With Jenna at a friend's and Robbie at Marian's, I decided to go to bed; I had barely slept in the past forty-eight hours. I walked down to my daughter's room and wrote in my journal about everything I could remember from the day. Things were happening that were bigger than me—they would also forever be a part of me—and I wanted to remember every detail.

I dropped my journal to the floor and lay back, looking up into the canopy circle above the bed. It flowed down with white gauzy material accented with pink and blue streamers. The puppies and kittens played and cuddled on the chair rail wallpaper border. The blue lattice wallpaper above and the pastel wallpaper below made me feel safe. I pushed away the mass of stuffed animals, and they plopped on the floor. I found Jenna's blanket, "Yellow," under her pillow. It was the blanket that Jenna first lay down on when she was brought home from the hospital. You could hardly call the shredded material a blanket, but the warmth it gave Jenna was beyond what a full-sized blanket could provide.

I nuzzled against Yellow as I prayed to God and the angels that when the time was right, they would take Ian quickly and painlessly. I drifted off to sleep.

I awoke in a most breathtaking place, surrounded by gleaming white and gold open-air buildings under a brilliant blue sky with shimmering clouds. People hurriedly scurried from one place to another preparing a huge feast. The whole scene oozed a palpable sense of excitement— there were so many souls running about.

An angel said, "Lisa, we are preparing for the arrival of the Great Ian Sharpe. We have been preparing for a long time, and the time is near for his brilliant soul to come and join us!" I had such a sense of euphoria at this moment. I noticed that an announcement was being repeated by another soul, a tall one, with two spirits following behind him who were gonging the most beautiful bell tones. "The Grand Mr. Ian Sharpe is about to arrive!" he exclaimed. The floors were gleaming clean marble; a sense of love surrounded everything. There was a thick feeling of anticipation among the group. It had to be heaven because it was like nothing on earth. I was caught up in the moment when trumpets sounded and then...

"Lisa, Lisa, wake up," I heard through the door. "We think Ian just passed away!"

I jolted awake, sat up and found myself tangled in the gauzy canopy. It was over my face and wrapped around one of my arms.

"Come in. Come in," I called.

Mike and Pierre almost fell into the room. It was 1:15 a.m.—I had been asleep for almost three hours. It was dark, and I was disoriented waking up in the middle of the night in my daughter's room. I patiently untangled myself and felt a sense of calm. I wasn't sure how I was going to

23

react when Ian died, but I sure didn't think it would be so peaceful. (I would learn the next day that at this same time, half way across the country in a small hotel room in a tiny town in Kansas, my mother, Judy, also had a dream about Ian. He'd come to say goodbye.)

I pushed past Mike and Pierre and ran down the hallway. The bedside lamp was the only light in the room. I ran up next to Ian, the oxygen still pushing clean fresh air into his lifeless lungs. I looked into his face—it was so clear that he wasn't there. He was a lifeless shell of himself. It was the same wan sunken face I had just kissed hours ago; yet the person, the soul I had kissed, was gone.

"What happened?" I asked softly.

Pierre said: "I was listening to the monitor, and Ian's breaths became more shallow and farther apart. So, I came upstairs and sat with him. His intake of breath was getting even farther apart and then it just stopped."

As is my way of dealing with things, I almost immediately focused on the next steps: *What do we do now? What about the kids? What about Ian's mother?* So many thoughts were racing through my head.

"We need to go make some calls," I said. "Could someone please get Ian's wedding ring off his finger?" I wanted to keep it. Mike stepped up to Ian's side of the bed and gently lifted his arm and grasped the ring and slid it off. He handed me the ring. I slipped it into my pocket.

We went downstairs and called the hospice nurse. It would take her a couple of hours to get there. I was so worried that the kids weren't going to be able to say goodbye to their dad. I called the funeral home. I explained that I wasn't ready for them to come and take his body yet. They understood and said to call back when I was ready.

I went upstairs alone to spend some time with Ian. The oxygen was still going, so when I got to the room, I took the plastic tubing out of his nostrils and gently took the tubing out from behind his ears. I then turned the machine off, which immediately deadened the room. I felt serene and grateful that the end had come swiftly. Just hours earlier, the hospice nurse told me he had no imminent signs of death and suggested it could be weeks or months before he died.

I went to turn off the electric blanket; Ian had been bone chillingly cold upon returning from Seattle. I reached for the control panel and on the display was the letter E. The usual settings were one through nine and H for high. I had never seen the letter E on it before and was very struck by it. I went downstairs and sat at the counter with Pierre.

I told Pierre about the E on the electric blanket. Pierre immediately said, "Eternity." I gasped and pulled the new wedding band from my pocket. Pierre didn't know anything about my Valentine's gift to Ian. Inside the band, I had engraved "Eternally Yours." Pierre and I looked at each other and smiled. Ian had told me that some way, somehow, he was going to send me a sign to let me know that he was okay. This was it.

The nurse arrived and pronounced Ian dead. She advised me to call the funeral home back and have them take the body as soon as possible.

I was so confused; I didn't know what to do. I called my friend Susie, who was a nurse, for guidance. She was skiing in Vermont, but had given me her phone number and told me to call if I needed anything. It must have been 3 a.m., but she was so supportive and helpful. She told me to call the funeral director and have them come get the body as it might be more upsetting to the kids to come home and see their dad dead in his bed. Also, his body would start to deteriorate which would be a traumatic thing for the children (and for me) to experience.

I hung up the phone and called Daniel Jowdy, the Kane Funeral Home director. He was at the house within the hour. Though it was the middle of the night, he was wearing the best-cut black suit I had ever seen and a gorgeous black wool overcoat. Behind him stood two more men who were faceless. Daniel spoke in a soothing yet respectful tone. However, he reminded me of the Angel of Death, almost *too* well put together; along with the two silent men standing behind him, the whole thing was eerie. Yet, in a vaguely comforting way, it reminded me of the dream I had had earlier that night.

I told Daniel that I was afraid the kids would be upset if Ian was gone and they didn't get a chance to say goodbye. He calmly said, "We cannot deny the children the privilege of saying goodbye to their father. I will make arrangements for an opportunity to view Ian's body later." I felt so relieved and walked Daniel and his helpers up to my bedroom. I went and sat on the couch in the family room. I didn't want to see them take Ian out on the stretcher.

When I went back up to my room, the funeral people had made my bed and even folded Ian's CAL blanket so that the insignia was right in the middle, a very respectful thing to do. It was treated as a holy spot, as someone had passed away there.

Afterwards, Mike, Pierre and I went back to bed; it was around 4:30 a.m. I slept for about two hours and then woke up and started writing in my journal. Around 7 a.m., I took a shower. While I was drying my hair, I had the hot air flowing on my face; I closed my eyes and I literally heard Ian whisper and felt his breath from behind my left ear. "Oh Lisa, I love you, but it is so awesome here!" I was startled, but then felt an enormous sense of peace. It was comforting to know that Ian was in a better place, especially since I had seen exactly where he was. I wasn't sad for Ian's passing, only sad for the rest of us who had to live on without him.

I braced to go tell the children and Ian's mother. Pierre and I drove over to Marian's, where Robbie had spent the night. Once Robbie came in I sat him on my lap and said, "Robbie, I'm so sorry. Daddy died last night."

Robbie wailed. "But I wanted to be with him one more night!" He was crushed, as was I for having to tell him. He cried and cried. It was beyond heartbreaking.

Mike and I then drove over to pick up Jenna from her sleepover. I walked in and took her to the side and as gently as I could said, "I'm so sorry honey, but Daddy died this morning at 1 a.m."

Jenna hardly blinked an eye and said, "Oh. Oh that's sad. Can I go tell my friends?" Had I not known my daughter so well, this reaction would have been perplexing. I said yes, so she trotted down to the basement and after gathering her things together, she casually said, "My dad died this morning." The three other girls gasped and went over to hug Jenna. Jenna was so like her father; she kept all emotion tucked deep inside. I hoped she would realize, sooner than later, that it was okay to let it out. Not only was it okay, it was a natural and healthy thing to do.

Later that day, Mike, Pierre and I took the kids to Kane Funeral Home. The funeral director explained to the kids that Daddy would be laying on a hospital gurney with a sheet covering him up to his chin. He explained that he had gone to heaven and this was just his body. The kids were scared and tentative. Jenna didn't want to go first, so Robbie and I went in. Robbie bravely walked right up to Ian and threw his arm over his chest. Then he reached up on his tiptoes and gave him a kiss on the cheek and then another hug. I could see that he was crying.

Jenna was standing at the door crying as well, so I went back and slowly walked forward with her. She was too scared; she wanted to say goodbye to her father, but just couldn't. I asked if she wanted me to give Daddy a hug and kiss for her, and she said yes, so I did. His body was stiff when I kissed him. His skin was cold and firm, like a watermelon. I stepped back and told Jenna to feel the table and that Daddy felt just like that. His body was a shell and had gone hard. She reluctantly stepped forward and gave him a big hug. She stayed for several seconds and just sobbed. It was the first time she had cried since hearing the news of Ian's death. We turned to leave, and she ran back to give Ian one last hug.

I was trying to comfort my sobbing kids as best as I could, as were Mike and Pierre. Daniel, the funeral director, had things I needed to sign.

"Thank you so much for making Ian look so good," I told him. "He looked beautiful."

"You're welcome, Mrs. Sharpe, but you are the hero here. The way you helped your children was incredible. This will be a moment they will never forget. I've seen many viewings and you were a rock." This reaction confounded me; I did just what I felt I should have done, nothing more and certainly nothing less.

I had never been so close to death before. When I was eleven, while I was visiting my dad's parents, my mother's father died. I didn't attend the service, and I really had no concept of death at the time. At age thirty-seven, I was now staring right at it; my own husband died in my bed early that morning, and now I had two young children to care for. And yet, the biggest thing I felt was relief. Seven years of endurance ended that February day. Ian was forty-four years old.

****

I think Ian chose his time. The kids were sleeping away from the house that evening; I was in another room, dreaming of heaven. He was in his own bedroom, where he felt safe. His best friend, Pierre, was sitting at his side listening to his belabored breathing. Ian felt peace. He felt safe. He felt love. He felt no guilt; so it was easy for him to simply let go.

He fought and he fought and he fought. Of course, he didn't want to leave us, but at some moment, he knew there was no other way, and he just let go. It was the perfect way in the perfect place. It was almost as if for the last twenty-four hours we had been set up in a magical chess game, and with each move we made we were one step closer to the ultimate checkmate.

CHAPTER 2

"*Oh, Lisa, I'm so sorry for your loss.*"
"*God doesn't give you more than you can handle.*"
"*Ian's in a better place, dear.*"

I dreaded going to the grocery store. I would inevitably run into someone who knew my situation.

I knew that people had the best intentions, but I just wanted to buy my frozen meatballs and jar of spaghetti sauce and get back home where I was safe. I began shopping in a neighboring town to avoid the endless stream of pitying glances and uncomfortable conversations. People didn't realize that I wanted privacy, yes, but also just some normalcy. I didn't want to have to face this heaviness every time I left the house. It was too overwhelming.

Three weeks after Ian's death, my mother and her husband invited the whole family on a Caribbean cruise— my brother, his wife and daughter, my children and me.

I knew getting away from the house and my well-meaning friends would be invigorating, something freeing after all the pain I had endured over the previous seven years. After the intensity of the past two years of nonstop doctors and hospitals, the act of flying to Florida and boarding a cruise ship was so incredibly foreign; I had no idea how to handle myself.

My life had been about Ian's illness for so long. Every moment was wrapped up in his cancer and his care. I was nurse, errand runner, medication expert, cancer researcher, confidante, bill payer, insurance agent, and chauffeur, not to mention a full-time mother and caregiver to our two young children. During Ian's illness, we'd endured three corporate moves to four houses in three states. In the final year of Ian's life, the insurance company wouldn't pay for his cancer treatments unless we sought care from their approved facility in Seattle. This required us to uproot the family from Connecticut to Washington State. We lived in a hotel room for over seven months while Ian underwent his final two stem-cell transplants. The stress and the heartbreak had been overwhelming for far too long. I needed a vacation, and my mother knew that.

One evening on the ship, the adults decided to go out for a special night and see a band in the Crow's Nest lounge. I couldn't remember the last time I had been excited about anything.

As I was dressing in my cabin, I wondered: How long had it been since I'd worn a dress, fixed my hair, and put on makeup and jewelry, all just for fun? I was just about to let myself embrace the idea when my mind flashed back to a heartbreaking moment from earlier that evening.

We were waiting in line to get our photo taken with the ship's captain. A sixty-something woman in a blue sequined evening gown approached my son. "Oh, young man, don't you just look so darn handsome?"

Robbie, in a blue blazer and a tie, proudly replied, "Thank you. My daddy died twenty-nine days ago. I got to wear it to the funeral."

The woman's face dropped, and her eyes went glassy. "Well, aren't you brave. I'm sure your dad is real proud of you."

I had to turn and look the other way.

Thinking back to this moment, I refocused my eyes on the mirror and allowed the wave of sadness to wash over me. The moment made it clear how much I needed a way to forget, if only for a little while.

Little did I know *how* that night would help me forget. From the moment the band started playing, the twenty-three–year-old lead singer had his eye on me. I was flattered. He was French Canadian with a fabulous accent. I couldn't remember the last time someone had flirted with me so overtly, or the last time I'd felt sexy. Having been in a type of prison for so long, I saw the light leading to the other side, and I just took off. And I kept running. I started to test the boundaries of my new freedom.

For the rest of the week, Luc and I flirted incessantly. The ship prohibited him from fraternizing with the passengers; it was no idle threat—he had seen fellow employees fired on the spot. So we had to sneak around, exchange looks, flirt without anyone seeing. I couldn't deny that the sneaking around itself was exciting. On the last night, we snuck to a dark corner of an outside deck. He was wearing a tuxedo, and I was wearing a sundress with a sweater. The moon's reflection danced off the dark ocean, and a breeze blew in renewed hope. Luc turned and kissed me. We wanted more, but there was no place to go.

We decided to sneak him into my room. We concocted an elaborate scheme of him tunneling through the worker's quarters and finding the employee's elevator nearest my room. He would then walk by at a precise time. I would open my door and let him duck inside.

I waited with shallow breath inside my door. At the prearranged time, I opened it. Luc quickly slipped inside. It worked! Not ten feet away lay my two sleeping children. I pulled the curtain closed between the sleeping area and the mini hallway. Like a couple of teenagers trying not to get caught, we began to silently kiss, but I was very nervous.

I opened the bathroom door, and we snuck inside. The room was tiny, just enough space for a toilet, a sink and a corner shower. After closing the door behind me, he put his finger to my lips and lunged forward. He kissed my neck and throat. His arm and chest muscles just melted me.

The kisses awakened me. I felt alive again for the first time in years. I ran my hands over his body and could tell he wanted more. My mind began to race through all the reasons to stop: *The kids were just on the other side of this thin wall. My husband had just died a month ago. I was fifteen years older than he was. What was I doing?*

Two opposing forces, equally strong, were tearing at me. Half of me felt guilty; the other half was so starved for affection that I was cherishing that moment as if it were my first kiss. It certainly *felt* as exciting as that first kiss.

I crossed over the line just enough to truly feel it. And then I stepped back behind it. Between my guilt, the concern about waking the children and his nervousness of being caught, we decided it was best if we ended our adventure. I ensured his tuxedo wasn't too rumpled, took a deep breath and slowly opened the bathroom door. The kids were sound asleep. I opened the exterior door and took a quick peek into the corridor to make sure he wouldn't be spotted. He walked out, and the next day we left the ship, with only our memories of that night.

I was scared to go home. For nearly a month, my mother and the rest of my family had been constantly at my side, both at home and on the ship. When I got back this time, I'd really be alone for the first time—the thought paralyzed me. I'd spent the last year and a half preparing for Ian's death with my therapist; we talked through the stages of grief, some of which I had experienced while Ian was still alive. Now that Ian was dead, I was simply lost. I didn't think I could go home and raise the children by myself. On one hand, I felt such a sense of relief that things were over, which I felt far too guilty about to express to anyone. I was also so pissed at Ian for leaving us. I knew he was gone, but I wasn't able to fully process it or face it. The thought of living on my own was just too terrifying to stare at directly.

Right away, I threw myself into all the things I couldn't seem to find time to do while Ian was sick: redecorating, landscaping, exercising, getting a new water heater, doing our taxes. As long as I kept busy, I knew I would be free from any pain. It had always been that way for me, and I took on my chores with a newfound verve.

Ian may have been gone, but it wasn't as if he didn't exist anymore. For one thing, strange electrical things kept happening in the house. Before he died, two new electric blankets hadn't been working, the garage door opener had been stuck, and the computer had been flickering, then suddenly after his death they all started working again. I was sure Ian was behind it all.

Two weeks after the cruise, I had to face my first holiday without him. It was the night before Easter, and I was lying in bed thinking about the Easter eggs. It was raining, and I was thinking how I would need to hide the brightly colored plastic eggs, filled with candy, coins and toys, in the house instead of in the yard. Ian was always in charge of the holidays. He loved them and went over the top in preparing for them.

He was the one who usually hid the eggs, and I loved him for that; now I was angry with him for not being there, for not handling all this. I didn't want to have to carry everything, but even more so, I didn't want to disappoint the kids. Hadn't they been through enough?

I looked out the window at the rain. When I turned back to the room, Ian was standing right there. I was stunned, I didn't move for fear he would disappear. He looked healed and healthy, his normal weight. I knew immediately that I was not imagining it; I was actually seeing his ghost. Seeing him was comforting and confusing at the same time. Yet, overall it felt like a gift, an amazing blessing that was unfolding right before my eyes. He stepped forward, gave me a big hug, and simply said telepathically, "Trust me." On the same night that Jesus rose from the dead, my husband returned.

After the hug, he went to lie down on the bed. Slowly, right before my eyes, he faded away. At first I was confused, but then I quickly felt comforted. I understood why he was there; he had just given me permission, not just about the Easter eggs, but to celebrate all things in my life in my own way.

In many ways with Ian's death, life became new. I wasn't tied down with the worry, despair, anger, and physical demands of caring for a dying person. I still had waves of grief from his loss, bad days mixed in with the good, but I also felt like now, finally, I could live life again.

Out of a need for routine, I began to regularly attend church again. I'd been going to the church since the first week we moved to Ridgefield, but I now felt differently about the place. During the moment of Ian's death, as I lay sleeping, I had dreamed of Ian in heaven. I knew in my soul that something had shifted for me spiritually. I was sure that church was no longer the answer for me, but I wasn't sure what was. I had to leave myself open to discover what would be next.

My new spiritual transition was still processing somewhere inside of me. I wasn't quite ready to let go of the church, which had served as my social base and connection to community. The people there knew my situation, and I felt their support rather than their unwanted pity. Yet, something had changed; I just didn't know what.

At church, I often would run into Steve. He was my age, good looking, and never married. I really didn't give him much thought until one day, about three months after Ian had passed, he was at my house helping me clean out the attic. When he left, he said, "If you ever need anything, call me, 24/7." That simple offer made me feel secure and hopeful. I realized I missed the protection and safety I'd felt with Ian at my side. From that moment on, I looked at Steve differently.

I decided to ask Steve if he would want to see a movie and grab a bite to eat. I figured I had known him for about six years; he was good with kids—as he was one of the youth leaders—and he was spiritual. When he agreed, my head started reeling with thoughts.

I felt it was difficult for friends and family to understand how quickly I wanted to date after Ian's death. I needed to feel alive, to feel excited, to have fun. Perhaps I was even a little crazy from the grief. I knew I wasn't thinking straight. On a spiritual level, I knew it was okay and that Ian was fine with it. Even if it was difficult for others to accept without judgment, I needed to live.

In my journal, I had specifically asked my angels for help in looking for a new husband. I loved being married and having a soul mate. I wasn't expecting it to happen right away, of course, but I wrote that I wanted a man who had never been married, had no kids, and someone who wasn't carrying around baggage. Both of my parents had been married twice after their divorce, and I didn't want my kids to have a similar experience as I did with various step siblings and ex-spouses. We had enough drama to deal with already. I was just looking for someone who would love and adore me and my children. I wanted my life back.

During dinner, Steve told me about his one and only love, a woman he'd met on a bus going to the airport. He seemed obsessed with her and not at all interested in anyone else, even though she apparently had no interest in him. Unfazed, he continued to pursue her to the exclusion of anyone else.

Because I was feeling a little unbalanced, I got it into my head that Steve would be the man for me, no matter how much the circumstances showed otherwise. Several days after our dinner, I impulsively told him that I had feelings for him, and I was hoping he did too.

He kindly said he didn't, but he would take things slow and see where it ended up. I was like a dog with a bone. I asked him to escort me to a going away party for two of my good friends, who were returning to California after seven years in Ridgefield. He said no problem.

A few days before the party, I tried calling to confirm, but he wouldn't return my calls. The night of the party, he stood me up. Having already booked the babysitter, and needing to get out, I decided to go on my own. It ended up being thirty-nine couples and me. I felt out of place, alone, and a little embarrassed.

After an hour, I called my friend Lisa. She had called me the night before and wanted to go out, but I didn't have a sitter. Lisa's husband had died of tongue cancer just two weeks after Ian died. We had met when Ian and I had first moved to town in 1996. Our kids had attended the same nursery school. Her husband had been the golf pro at the local private country club for twenty-two years before he passed away.

"Hey, do you want to go out tonight? I'm already out of the house and the kids are home with a sitter. Steve is such an ass! He said he'd take me to a going away party for two of my friends. I have to get out of here, but I really don't want to go back home after only an hour."

She agreed. We decided to go to the new bar in town, Upstream. It had been open for a week, and it was the trendy place to go. The room was packed, and the music was blaring. We pushed our way to the bar, found some stools and ordered some strawberry martinis.

Lisa leaned toward me and yelled, "Hey, the new golf pro is here! Let me introduce you."

"Sure," I said, only half hearing her.

Lisa waved to a handsome man at the other end of

the bar. He was standing behind three rows of people trying to get the bartender's attention. As she was waving, he looked behind himself to see if she was waving to someone else. He finally realized that he was the one being waved to, and he slowly inched his way down to where we were sitting.

Lisa screamed into my ear, "Lisa, this is David Jones!"

I turned around to shake hands and nearly fell off the barstool. The din around me faded, and I stared right into him. Everything went blurry, but he remained in focus. He was gorgeous; his eyes were a mesmerizing blue. He then spoke with an Irish accent, which floored me. When we shook hands, a shock of electricity went up my arm.

David waved his three friends over to join us. One of the guys was all over me. He leaned over toward my stool, put his arm around me, and began telling me all about his problems with his kids and ex-wife. He continued to slur his words and hang on my shoulder. I excused myself to go to the ladies' room with Lisa.

As soon as we got into the bathroom, Lisa asked me what I thought of David. She said he was single and had never been married. I was a high school girl again; I giggled and told her to give him my number.

At the end of the evening, I asked if anyone had change so I could pay my babysitter. David pulled out a wad of bills and broke my twenty. He asked me how old my kids were. I told him, and was relieved that he knew about my kids; he didn't seem at all put off by it. Dating was completely foreign to me. I didn't want to hide anything, but I also didn't want to reveal too much either. Learning to strike a balance would take time. I had been away from this game for quite some time.

On my way home, my mind floated back to the first time I laid eyes on Ian. It was my first day of work in the tax department at Price Waterhouse. I had moved to San

Francisco after college with the sole intention of focusing intently on my career—dating was not on my agenda. However, when Ian Sharpe walked through the conference room door, out of nowhere, I thought: "Now there's a guy I could marry." It was love at first sight. Tonight, with David, the exact same thing had happened; *I just knew.* Was it clarity or craziness? I didn't know anything about David, but the moment I turned around on that stool and we looked each other in the eye, I got that same feeling. It was all happening so fast, and I joyfully jumped onboard. There was no way I was going to let it pass me by.

I was fine with this sudden turn, happy to embrace what was in front of me. But I was nagged by another question: *What would other people think?*

CHAPTER 3

Monday, June 21, 2004

A s summer was approaching the year Ian died, I decided to do something out of the ordinary. The kids' birthdays were a week apart in December. I decided instead to celebrate their *half-*birthdays with a big outdoor summer bash at the house. I knew experiencing our first Christmas without Ian was going to be excruciatingly difficult, especially because Ian loved organizing the holidays, and the idea of creating two birthday parties during the holiday season was not something I wanted to think about.

So I decided to throw the half-birthdays in June, a thinly veiled attempt to bring joy and normalcy back into our lives. Their school gym teacher came and put together a giant outdoor obstacle race. I rented two huge inflatable castles for the kids to bounce and slide on. For dessert, I made arrangements for the Lickety-Split Ice Cream Truck to come to the house, so all thirty party guests could choose their own treat.

As I was leaving the grocery store that day, grabbing some last minute items, my cell phone rang.

"Hey, Lisa. It's David Jones. We met at Upstream the other night."

My heart took off racing. I knew exactly who it was, where I had met him, and when. But I couldn't let on how I excited I was—I was a schoolgirl again, pretending to be casual.

"Hi. Yes, hi. I remember." I kept the excitement as bottled as I could.

"I was wondering what you were up to today? It's my day off. I thought we might get together for coffee."

"I'd love to, but actually I'm at the grocery store. I'm throwing a birthday party for my kids."

"Oh, wow, it's *their* birthday? They're twins?"

I explained to David the half-birthday idea, which sounded a little outlandish when I said it aloud. "Would you be free this evening? I could see if I could get a sitter?"

There was a slight pause, a canyon of time, then he replied: "Sure. Tonight works."

"Great."

I was already counting down the hours, thinking what I'd wear.

He said, "Oh, by the way. Turn around."

"What?" I stopped loading my groceries into my car and turned to look over my shoulder. David was driving toward me in the parking lot. "Oh my goodness—what are you doing here?" I said, closing my phone.

He stopped and got out. "I was leaving the Radio Shack over there when I called. Let me give you a hand."

David picked up the last two bags and placed them in the trunk of my car. We chatted a bit and decided to meet that night at Eastridge Cafe for drinks.

The faux birthday party was a huge success— except for the confusion regarding the kids' ages. I guess the half birthday idea was peculiar to people. The best part of the event was simply being outside and seeing the kids play in the rich sun, a treat that my winter-born children never get to experience on their birthdays. I liked the change, especially after the year we'd had. The kids had been through so much, and I could see on their faces that it was a welcome break. They deserved it.

After the last child was picked up and Jenna and Robbie were in the house playing with their new gifts, I walked to the end of the yard, picking up ice cream wrappers and popped balloons. When I turned back toward the house, I froze in amazement. I spotted four flowering sapphire irises behind a large rock. Everything stopped, movie-like; then the background became blurry and the flowers came into sharp focus.

I had never seen those flowers in our yard before.

That day would have been Ian's and my twelfth wedding anniversary, which of course I knew, but I had tried not to think too hard about it. The flowers were his way of acknowledging it. I had the most beautiful and poignant reminder of the day's importance, and of our life together. A gift from somewhere else entirely; I was both shaken and comforted. I felt like Ian had placed these flowers, my favorite kind, exactly in that spot on this day as a gift for me.

Later, I made arrangements for our neighbor's son to come over and watch the kids. I had recently purchased a few new things to wear, as my wardrobe over the past few years had been reduced to "caretaker chic." I wore a casual sweater set with crop pants and wedge sandals. It felt so good to be out of my normal baggy sweatpants, jeans and oversized shirts. Sometimes when your life is out of whack it's the little things you miss the most.

I drove Ian's convertible the five miles to the center of town. I was feeling excited and nervous as I approached the cafe, maybe a bit guilty about driving Ian's car to a date with someone else. I reminded myself that it was okay, that Ian was in a wonderful place and invested in my happiness. The flowers were the perfect reminder of this.

The restaurant, a quaint New England-style building with white clapboard siding and two dormers on the roof, was on the corner of two busy streets. On both sides of the front door was an outdoor patio with white picket fencing. As I approached the door, I saw David chatting with a group of guys on the patio. He was effortlessly handsome in jeans, a polo shirt, and loafers. His short brown hair looked freshly washed, and his blue eyes smiled warmly. We met eyes and David excused himself from the crowd to welcome me. Here I was, dating again. The anticipation turned my stomach to jelly.

After we sat down, David ordered a beer, and I asked for a Grey Goose dirty martini with three olives. Then everything just opened up naturally. I couldn't help but watch David across the table. His face lit up as he smiled, the creases highlighting his blue eyes. I noticed how strong his hands were as he gripped his beer glass. Trying not to get lost in him, I focused on asking questions.

"So when did you come to America?"

"Let's see...1989. I won the lottery."

"No! *Really?*"

He laughed. "No, not that kind of lottery. A Donnelly Visa—it gives a working visa for the U.S. to a set amount of people. It's random, like a lottery. There were about nineteen million applicants the year I got it, from thirty-something countries. I think they issued about ten thousand visas the year I got mine."

"That's incredible."

"It was. It is." His look was bearing right into me when he said this. There was a slight pause. Not uncomfortable, but a bit heavy. To fill it, I said the first thing I could think of. "So when did you get into golf?"

His eyes beamed open at this question—it was clear that he loved answering it. "Well, when I was as a kid, I used to sneak onto the fairway behind my house in Dublin, so I could practice. I just loved it, more than anything else.

Over time, people started to notice me, but I never did much with it. I never pursued it. When I got here, I worked in the car rental industry for a couple of years, did pretty well in it, too. I was put in a management-training program. To be honest, it just wasn't for me. It didn't *do* anything for me, I should say. So, I walked away to pursue my passion."

"Wow. That's bold. I'm impressed. So many people are too afraid to do that."

"Thanks. It felt like an easy choice, in a way."

I loved the way he spoke. It was magnetic.

David continued, "Looking back, I guess one day I just made the decision to quit my job, and then I started showing up at the Westchester Country Club and asking if they needed a caddy."

I laughed. "Oh my goodness. I love it!"

"The first day, the caddy master told me to get lost, but I just wouldn't listen. Two more times I showed up; two more times he told me to get lost."

"Persistent."

"Yes. You could call it a lot of things. Anyway, on the fourth attempt, they were short caddies, and I got my chance. After having caddied for a short time, there was a job opening in the bag room, which I managed to get. And then I was on my way."

He worked his way up the golf club circuit, first as an assistant at various clubs and then landing two head pro jobs in and around Westchester County, New York. After several years in the industry, he found himself as the head golf professional at Silver Spring Country Club.

My friend Lisa's husband, Stan Garrett, was the golf pro at Silver Spring when David first worked there. Stan had needed support to help run the golf operation due to his illness. After Stan's death, David became the head professional. It seemed a bit crazy, but things were aligning in a way that I just couldn't deny. Everything had been following a certain beautiful path.

I told David about Ian, his long battle with cancer and how he had died that February. He asked just the right questions, clearly understanding how sensitive it was to talk about. With some people, it was easier not to get into it. But not David. He empathized, both because of who he was and because he had been through something similar.

David had gone back to Ireland to care for his father, who had also passed away from cancer. He'd take the morning shift and go to the hospital at 7 a.m., staying until 3 p.m. He would sit by his dad, whose tracheotomy made it impossible for him to talk, eat or drink. They would pass a notebook back and forth to communicate. David assisted the hospital staff in nursing his father—bathing, feeding and even cleaning his trach tube.

When Lisa introduced us, she mentioned his dad had also just died of cancer, but I hadn't realized David had been such an intimate caregiver. I could not believe the unity of such a personal experience that we shared with each other. Our connection became that much deeper. Sitting at that table, I felt that David's entrance into my life must have been fated. David was the only one I could've been with after Ian, someone who understood the heavy weight that comes with caring for a loved one and then losing that person to the ugliness of cancer.

I seemed to see cancer everywhere, both before and after Ian's death. I felt like I didn't know anyone who hadn't been touched by the disease. To this day, as I talk to more and more people, I continue to feel that way.

As the sunlight began to fade, we continued talking. We each ordered a glass of wine and things got even more intimate. He explained that he had no intention of asking me out when he discovered I was a widow.

"Really?" I asked.

"Well, my sister's husband died of a sudden heart attack almost exactly a year ago. Left her with five children, all young. I saw what that did to her. *Up close*, I saw it. I can't imagine what she would have thought if some guy asked her out so soon after losing her husband. I didn't want to take that chance with you."

"Okay." I didn't know what to make of this. "So what changed your mind?"

He gave me a knowing look. "I think you told me to call, right? I mean you told Lisa?"

I went shy all of sudden. "Guess I'm guilty there." I couldn't put into words what I was really thinking. After having a sick husband for seven years, I felt as though I had done a lot of grieving. I was ready to be happy and have some fun again. It was just too hard to say out loud or even try to put that into words. I let the thought pass.

"Well, I'm glad you did."

"Me too."

I asked him about his family. He told me he had four brothers and two sisters. Two brothers lived in London, and the others were still in Ireland, near Dublin. He told me how his mom was going to be moving into a granny flat they were building onto his sister's house.

Of course, I was more than curious about his views on kids. If anything, it was an enormous deciding factor in whether or not we continued on this path. My kids were young and going to be in the picture for a while. It was too important for it to remain a mystery, so I just dove into it.

"Have you thought about kids?" I asked.

"Sure. I've always wanted kids. Two, actually." I might have audibly exhaled when he said that. "But," he added, "I never wanted to do the 'baby' thing."

"*Okay*...how exactly does that work?"

He laughed. "I'm not really sure how that part will work. *Yet.* I do know that I want to have a son and name him Robert. That way I'd have a Bobby Jones, just like the famous golfer." He smiled.

I could barely breath. He had no idea that my son's name was Robert. I was having a hard time putting all the pieces together. It felt too good to be true. Usually when things feel that way, they are, but this time things were feeling really right. It was as though I had conjured up the ideal person to lead me back into the rest of the world, the world not consumed by Ian and sickness and the tough years I had just gone through.

I told David that it would have been Ian's and my twelfth anniversary that day. He slid his hand across the table and gave my hand a squeeze. I went on to tell him about how I was adopted at birth, my life growing up in Colorado, moving all over the country for Ian's job and how I was pursuing my dream of being an actress. These were things that I usually didn't blurt out after first meeting someone. There was something about the way he focused on me and listened that made me want to tell him more.

At the end of the evening, David walked me to my car. I was feeling so alive and connected that I kissed him with more force and zeal than I probably should have. I was just so damn happy.

He whispered in my ear, "Happy anniversary."

That brought me back to earth, but it also showed me what a caring, sweet man he was.

He called my cell a few minutes after I arrived at my house.

"I just wanted to be sure you made it home okay."

I was swooning. "Thanks, I did. Goodnight. Thanks for calling."

"'Night."

I paid the sitter and checked on the kids, who were sleeping soundly after such a busy day. I got my journal out and re-read what I had written two months earlier:

Dear Angels,
Please help me find a man that will love me
for who I am as well as my children, as if
they were his own. I want someone who has

never been married, and has never had children. I'm looking for someone with no baggage, ideally someone in his late thirties who is caring, loving and giving. Thank you.

I was almost numb from the evening I'd had; David seemed to have met all the criteria I had asked for and more. I imagined Ian, David's father Declan, and Stan, who had all died of cancer in the last six months, having a pint of Guinness in heaven, choreographing my meeting with David. It all seemed surreal; I couldn't have invented something that felt more perfect.

****

The next day, the kids and I went on a road trip to New Jersey to visit some old friends. Throughout the week, David was texting and calling me, like a high school boyfriend. I had never texted before, so my friends helped me to figure out how to reply to his little notes. I have to admit that it was thrilling having someone to look forward to hearing from. I had gone from feeling so old for my age—because of my time as caretaker and Ian's death—to feeling half my age, because of how David made me feel.

David and I met two more times the following week, recognizing that fate and circumstance were dragging us faster along than we would've planned—but not faster than we both liked. I was falling for him, and I would've been lying to myself if I pretended otherwise. I really didn't care about the impression that outsiders might have of it. I knew what I knew and I had been through enough not to concern myself with perception. This was it. This was real.

One night, we were at his apartment, and we were about to make love for the first time. Again, the two opposing forces were pulling at me. I could literally feel both sides tugging. One side argued that I had just lost my husband and how could I even possibly consider getting involved so soon. The other side told me what I had always known: *I had been starved for affection for years.* During the time Ian was sick, being intimate was not a high priority. A lot of the time, it wasn't even possible.

Even as David and I were walking to his bedroom, I wasn't sure I was ready. But then the thought ran through my head: If I said no and I died in a car accident on my way home, I would never get to make love to this beautiful man, this man who was so kind and seemed to know me so well already. A man that *I* desired to make love to. That made my decision. I didn't take the next day for granted. It was strange, but Ian's death taught me something that helped me move forward with David.

David and I continued to see each other as much as possible. He was very busy with running the golf course, and I was consumed with the kids' schedules. Somehow we managed to meet on a regular basis.

That Christmas, the kids, David and I went to Denver to visit my family. We stayed at my brother's house. His wife, Wendy, and his daughter, Kara, were there, as were my mom and stepdad who had flown in from Minneapolis. The day after Christmas, we were in the kitchen, when David came in and made an announcement: "I'd like everyone to know that Lisa saved my life today."

Everyone turned around.

"What?" my brother asked.

"Before Lisa invited me to come to Denver, my plan was to go to Phuket, Thailand, with a buddy of mine for the holidays. Neither of us ended up going."

I had no idea where this was going. "David, how…"

"I just saw the news. There was a giant tsunami. They're estimating that over two hundred and fifty thousand people were swept out to sea and killed." David was visibly shaken. "I would have been there."

We were dumbfounded. Later we watched the news and were overwhelmed with the amount of devastation unfolding before our eyes, the cameras, and the horrified world. I didn't make any announcement, but I could have said the same thing that day: My life was also saved with David's choice to not go to Phuket.

CHAPTER 4

A s a child I dreamed of being famous, of being photographed and having my face plastered on the covers of grocery store magazines. I wanted to be on a popular TV show or on the big screen. I wanted to be in the spotlight.

My brother and I were adopted. Eric, twenty-two months older than me, was adopted in California. My family moved to Colorado, where they adopted me when I was days old. I was the product of a one-night stand between a sorority girl and a fraternity boy at the University of Colorado, Boulder, in 1966.

Growing up, I didn't know about the one-night stand; I had the fantasy that my birth parents were Hollywood film stars. I was convinced they met on a movie set and fell in love. The problem, as I invented it, was they were both married to other people, like Liz Taylor and Richard Burton. The actress decided to go on hiatus and deliver me in seclusion. She gave me up for adoption and returned to Hollywood without anyone being the wiser.

The reality of my birth parents' story was far less glamorous. My birth mother became a teacher, married someone else and had three other children. My birth father became a state government employee, married two or three times and had two other daughters. I learned this many years later when I met them both in my late twenties.

I'm sure the fantasy about my birth parents was what gave me a desire to perform—the idea that I was a product of movie stars just seeped into my brain. In the sixth grade, I had the part of Thomas Edison's teacher in a play. Putting on the gray scratchy wig and filling my costume with a buxom bosom allowed me to be bold and daring. It was fun to pretend to be someone else and fantastic to feel like the star of the show.

I also loved watching Phil Donohue. I'd imagine sharing my story on his stage. Even better was to imagine that when he retired I would take over as host. *Gilligan's Island* was another favorite; I would imagine myself interacting with Gilligan, the Skipper, and all the other castaways. I also loved *Family Affair* and fantasized about being invited to play with Buffy and Jody in their glamorous New York City apartment. It would always end with Mr. French bringing us some fabulous dessert.

In high school, I didn't get involved with the theater crowd. I still held onto my desire to be in the movies or on TV, but I secretly feared the task of memorizing all of the lines. I decided I would be better off pursuing my dream later in life.

Being a people-pleaser, as well as a "good girl," I muted my own desires and continued on in my life according to the blueprint my father and stepmother imposed on me.

They were both very vocal about me getting a business degree, which I ultimately achieved, after some major angst. The desire to be in the spotlight was still within me, but it was buried, pushed out of the way to make room for more practical choices.

****

In 1996, after my marriage to Ian, the birth of our two children and moving around the country from Denver to San Francisco to Washington D.C. to Hartford, Connecticut and ultimately to Ridgefield, Connecticut, I finally had a chance to try my hand at acting again. Ian's job had been taking us all over the country, preventing me from pursuing my own interests up to that point.

The church I joined decided to produce some plays as part of their community outreach. I was cast as an angel in *Everyman*. I was thrilled to be in it, even though it was a small part. The show had big talent. The director was a playwright and co–artistic director of an off-Broadway theater and several of the actors had extensive TV and movie experience. Even around talented well-known actors and directors, I felt at home.

Despite my small part, my connection to the world of performance felt solid. A year later, I was cast as the first priest in the church's production of *Murder in the Cathedral* by T.S. Eliot. Terrell Anthony, who played Rusty Shayne for eighteen seasons on *Guiding Light*, was also in the play. We became friends; he encouraged me to take classes, to tap into my commercial look, and even to explore voice-overs. It was just the boost I needed. I decided to put more effort into honing my craft.

And then, everything ground to a halt; Ian was diagnosed with cancer. My acting was put on hold as were a lot of other things in our lives. After a year of treatment and a promotion with GE Capital, which involved moves to Ohio and New Jersey, Ian went into remission. However, we were no longer near New York City, where it was easier to pursue my acting. Life moved on.

And so did we. In January of 2001, GE moved us back to Ridgefield, Connecticut. After moving eight times by our eighth year of marriage, I thought I would enjoy working in the real estate industry, as I had so much first-hand experience in this field. When we had sold our home in Ridgefield in 1998 and again when we moved back in 2001, we had worked with one of the top performing real estate professionals in town. I mentioned to him that I would be interested in working on his team, as I loved the buying and selling experience. He already had a full-time assistant, but he agreed to hire me to help with the automation of his office.

After being "behind the curtain" of this powerhouse realtor for a very short time, I realized that he didn't get there by being the congenial person he projected to the public. He got there by being the most aggressive marketer in the town, a backroom politician with other realtors, and a master of persuasion to both buyers and sellers. It was not at all what I thought it would be; it was intense pressure. After four months, I couldn't stomach being in that environment. By then I had my real estate license, so I left him and joined Weichert Realty. The second day of my training, which was in Rockland County, NY, was September 11, 2001.

I had carpooled with another woman from the office. When we arrived at the training facility at 9 a.m., people were talking about a plane hitting the twin towers. We all thought it had been a small plane that had crashed, a pilot error or some kind of freakish mistake. Once we found out what happened, the class was dismissed.

As we drove home, we crossed the Tappan Zee Bridge over the Hudson River, and we could see the World Trade Center in the distance. A plume of smoke and debris burst from the towers. Planes were darting in the skies above. We were stuck in bumper-to-bumper traffic. We weren't sure what was going on; it was chaos. We worried the jets might dive-bomb into the bridge. It was terrifying.

After getting back to my house, I drove to the elementary school where my kids were. Like a lot of mothers that day, I wanted my children close. As we drove home, the kids asked me why they had to leave school.

"Mom, why did you pick us up? I missed recess," Robbie, then in kindergarten, asked.

"I just want you home with me. Some crazy things are happening, and I want you to come home. Daddy is coming home from work too."

"My teacher told us that some planes hit the big towers in New York. My friend Jack, his dad works in one of the towers," Jenna said, eager to share her news.

I had no idea the school had told the children what was going on. The emotion in me began to rise. Tears sprang to my eyes.

"It's okay, Mom. He'll just get a new daddy," she said. She couldn't yet fathom the death of her own father. I couldn't stop the tears. The naiveté and innocence of children is precious and yet heartbreaking at the same time.

That day changed a lot of things—both big and small, both directly and indirectly. Needless to say, the real estate business was at a standstill for almost six months after the 9/11 attacks. During this slow time, I became good friends with Lee, one of the realtors who had been in the business for many years. She suggested that we read *Dr. Robert Anthony's Advanced Formula for Total Success* to increase our real estate sales. I would not be exaggerating to say that the book changed my life. I read and reread it until it was dog-eared and covered in highlights. It opened everything up to me, giving me confidence and leading me down the path to follow my passion.

The book helped me see that I didn't have to do what other people expected of me; I could do what I wanted with my life. It woke me up. I'd spent my life conforming. I did not want to sell real estate; I wanted to be an actress! It was ironic that a book that I picked up to help me in one career led me to another.

In the spring of 2002, I signed up for classes at the Weist-Barron Acting School for Television in Manhattan. I took their Basic and Advanced Commercial classes and received encouraging remarks from all of the teachers. I then took voice-over classes and additional training at the Howard Meyer Acting Program.

Again, opposing forces tugged at me. Though it was such an exciting time in my life, this was also when Ian was re-diagnosed with cancer. On our tenth anniversary in 2002, we went to Bermuda for a week to celebrate. While we were there, Ian started having night sweats and fevers. His night tremors were so bad his shaking would wake me up. The celebration was bittersweet, as we knew he needed to go in for testing once we got home.

The doctor didn't mince words: "The cancer is back. Given that using your own stem cells four years ago didn't hold, I would suggest a transplant using donor cells."

I knew intuitively this was not going to end well.

While Ian navigated another course of debilitating chemotherapy, I continued on my acting path. I had headshots taken and the next thing I knew I was called to be a bride on the one-hundredth episode of *Will & Grace,* the hottest sitcom on NBC at that time. I connected with an agent who was sending me out on auditions in New York, Boston and Connecticut. I was involved with several corporate videos (including one for GE), training videos (including one for Friendly's Ice Cream) and various manufacturing videos. I also had a guest shot with Barbara Walters on *The View* when she shot a promo in the audience; she sat beside me and we chatted. I was continually surprised at how acting opportunities came out of the blue for me.

The acting experiences that came my way were thrilling and a wonderful escape; however, Ian's illness always brought me back to reality. As soon as the *Will & Grace* episode wrapped for the day, I was the first one to the dressing room, to change out of the wedding dress. I drove from Central Park to Sloan Memorial Kettering Hospital to pick up Ian's most recent CAT scan, which showed the spread of his disease. Like so many moments over Ian's last years, the good was always sliced quite pointedly by the bad.

The next big break came when one of my acting school buddies was cast as a butler in an independent feature film, a psycho-thriller called *Taffy Was Born*. The actress that played Cecelia, a small but pivotal role, had been fired a week before filming. The director asked the cast and crew if they knew of an actress in her late thirties with blond hair, blue eyes, and a slight build who would be available to start shooting in Connecticut the following weekend. Luckily for me, my friend recommended me, and I was offered the part. It was another serendipitous opportunity, and I grabbed it. In acting, you take what you can get—you never know when the offers will dry up or what something will lead to. We filmed over several weekends that fall and wrapped in late winter.

Unfortunately, Ian was getting worse. Our health insurance company decided that it would be best if we packed up our family and went to Seattle for four months so Ian could undergo treatment at the Fred Hutchinson Cancer Care Alliance. We ended up staying seven months at a Marriott Residence Inn there, as Ian needed two stem-cell transplants instead of one. The care and support we received in Seattle was phenomenal. They even had a school for the children to attend. All the pupils were either children or siblings of patients or patients themselves. We met so many wonderful friends during our stay. It made the hardship of that time more bearable.

One of the highlights was participating in events at Gilda's Place, an organization that supports cancer patients and their families while they are coping with the illness. They offered free yoga classes, Pilates, lectures, group sessions, as well as kids' activities. One of the lectures they presented was about feng shui, the study of the placement of objects in your environment to purposefully influence the way your life works. Initially, I was overwhelmed with all the information. With time and patience, I slowly learned this ancient art and started putting it to use in my life. Over time it literally changed the way I lived.

To start, I had the kids help me feng shui the areas in their hotel room, while I worked on the rest of our space. In the kids' room, for example, the closets were all mirrors. We covered the mirrors with blankets so they would sleep better. We added family photos into the family section of the hotel room and within hours we received the first phone call from Ian's mother since we'd arrived in Seattle. We put amethyst crystals in the wealth area and out of the blue we received a bonus check. I immediately saw a difference in the way everything was flowing in our lives.

My agent continued to call. When we had to extend our stay in Seattle beyond the initial four months, I asked her to stop calling, as it was too difficult to know what I was missing out on. Deep down I was beginning to have mixed feelings about my acting career. I felt like something was missing, but I couldn't put my finger on what it was. At this point it was easiest not to think about it.

The doctors sent us home in late November 2003. The cancer was continuing to spread and nothing more could be done. I felt the hospital didn't want Ian dying while under its care, as their success statistics would go down.

Ian would die in February—just four months later.

****

After the kids and I returned from our Caribbean cruise at the end of March, I started making plans to keep myself busy. I signed up for Pilates training three times a week. I also called a professional feng shui consultant to have my home evaluated and to see what I had to do to enhance the energy in order to improve my situation.

The practitioner, Joanne, came to my home and helped me to move my things around so that the energy in the house would be the most advantageous for me and the children. My two main goals were to help us move forward in our grief and to reignite my acting career, which I saw as a source of happiness and hopefulness in my life. In the back of my mind, I wanted to ultimately remarry, but that wasn't the primary concern.

The consultation was everything I had hoped for and more. We walked through each room, and Joanne gave me suggestions on where to place my furniture, pictures and accessories, as well as what types of items I should purchase to make the energy flow better. She told me where to put photos of Ian, to help with our grief. When it came to the "fame/reputation" section, she suggested that I add a bouquet of red flowers, as this would pull the energy to my acting career. In regard to the "love" section, it was all about clearing the space of any old, stagnant energy and allowing fresh, clear energy to enter.

Within about a month of Joanne's visit, I received news that *Taffy Was Born* was selected for the LA Film Festival in October. I was ecstatic. Since arriving back home from Seattle, and Ian's death in February, I had had no time, energy or desire to get back to the acting, but this piece of news brightened my outlook. About twelve weeks after I had the house feng shuied, I met David. Between talking to my angels and remaking my living space, things began to turn around for me.

As the October date for the LA Film Festival was approaching I had no desire to attend. However, just days before the screening, the director informed us that *Taffy Was Born* was selected to be shown at the Cannes Film Festival in France the following May! I immediately made arrangements for someone to watch my kids and booked a flight to Los Angeles. I had no intention of missing out on the beginning of this next adventure.

A few months later, I asked a neighbor friend to join me on my journey to the Cannes Film Festival. Pattie and I had met at a neighborhood newcomer's party when Ian, the kids and I moved back to Ridgefield in 2001. In retrospect, I'm not sure what prompted me to invite her, since we weren't close at that time; I just intuitively felt we would get along and have a lot of fun. Pattie had recently decided to go back to school to get her nursing degree. She has an elegant ease about her, which made her the perfect traveling companion for this high-fashion event.

Due to Pattie's exam schedule, we had to book a flight, that if all went according to plan, would barely give us enough time to be on time for the movie screening. We arrived in Nice, on the French Riviera, and drove north to our hotel in Cap d'Ail on the border of Monaco. We double-parked the car, checked into the hotel, quickly showered, and changed into our glamorous eveningwear. We then jumped back into the car, found the highway and sped south to Cannes.

As we drove, it hit us that we had no idea *where* in Cannes the festival was located. The next hour felt chaotic—we rode on pure instinct toward the center of town. We looked for signs and somehow found our way to an entrance with an automated gate. The arm of the gate was down. Had we come all this way, only to miss the screening?

As we pondered what to do, a car entered in front of us. I stepped on the gas, and we cleared the gate just as it was coming down behind us. We parked, got out and smoothed our outfits. Because of our late arrival, we did not have our credentials to get into the theater.

"Pretend like we know exactly what we are doing and where we are going," I told Pattie.

We held our heads high, and walked past security at the back of the complex. The adrenaline rush was incredible. A program, handed to us, indicated the location

LISA JONES

of the screening area. After an escalator ride and a long walk down a corridor, we were nearly there. As I reached for the handle to enter the theater, a security guard grabbed my arm. He demanded our passes. Fortunately, the director, David Giardina, was inside and had our documentation. We had made it! As the film began to play, first Pattie, and then I promptly fell asleep, we were exhausted.

After the screening, we were able to walk out on the red carpet. It was surreal; just like the time I played Thomas Edison's teacher, I once again felt like a star. There were paparazzi snapping pictures and people asking for autographs. Afterwards, Pattie and I went with David to have dinner. She and I then spent a week enjoying the sights of Cap d'Ail and Monaco. The weather was perfect and the experience was incredible.

All of the buildup, the exciting arrival and then...it was all over.

The drop off came quickly. That August I was cast for a national commercial, which required me to fly to Los Angeles for the shoot. This experience turned out to be extremely negative, especially after the high of Cannes that prior May. To begin, I found myself waiting hours at the hotel for the driver. After arriving at the location site, I found myself again waiting for hair and makeup and then another long wait to finally be filmed for the commercial. I felt like a prop. I wasn't allowed to *be me*. I was told what to say and how to say it and ultimately if "they" (the director, the producer, or the client) didn't like the way I looked or how I said something, I was done.

Meanwhile, the kids and David (we were now engaged) were back in Connecticut. I wanted to be with them and be a family—not waiting around on a film set. I still wanted to be on stage to let my light shine, but I just couldn't do it under these conditions. When I returned home, I asked my agent not to call anymore. Acting went from something that made me feel like a star to something

63

that treated me like an object. That's the strange thing about the acting work; sometimes you're one, sometimes you're the other. It was then that I realized why deep down I had mixed feelings. I just wanted to be me. It wasn't worth it to ever not be me, so I left the business for good. There had to be other ways to get that rush, that feeling that I mattered—I was on the lookout to find what they were.

CHAPTER 5

I remember the very first time I discovered the secret to connecting directly with God. I was six and living in Minnesota with my family while my father pursued his doctoral degree.

It happened at a YMCA summer day camp. One of the male camp counselors, a gangly guy about sixteen, started bouncing a rubber dodge ball off the top of my head. I would scream every time he did it, but he thought it was funny. Once I realized he wasn't going to stop, my fight-or-flight instincts kicked in, and I took off running, darting toward the YMCA building. He chased after me. I was terrified; I didn't know what he would do to me if he caught me, and I had no interest in finding out.

I entered the building, looked back and saw he was still coming. I ran into the ladies' locker room, positive that he would follow me in. I spotted an open locker and climbed inside. Putting my back to the wall, I slid down to my butt, brought my knees to my chest and pulled the door shut. Then I barely breathed—I just sat there in sheer terror, the kind you can only feel as a little kid. After a few minutes, I realized that he wasn't coming in. I was relieved until it hit me that no one else would be coming in either.

I was trapped in the locker.

I pounded on the thin metal door with my hands and started to scream, "Help me! Let me out!" Once I heard my voice and realized how alone it sounded, the panic started to set in. It was the end of the day, and no one was there. My heartbeat was deafening, and I didn't know what to do. I started to kick the door with my right foot. After some time I was able to get my foot pushed out between the door and the locker frame. By bashing the bottom of the door, I managed to bend it open. My leg moved in and out, but the door still remained latched. I was completely trapped.

After ten minutes of screaming, kicking and pounding, the energy started to drain out of me. It was only when I finally stopped fighting that I began to calm down. In the quiet, my mind was free to wander and seek. I remembered something my Sunday school teacher had told me a few days earlier:

"If you ever need help, you can always ask God."

I took a deep breath, and put my hands into a prayer position. I spoke aloud, my tiny voice an echo in those metal walls of the locker: "Dear God, please, please help me get out of here."

A calm rose from my stomach and a wave of love washed over me. I heard a voice in my head: *Look down and press the metal rod up.*

I looked down and saw a round silver rod that ran from the top of the locker door. I could see that the rod didn't go all the way to the bottom. I dropped my right hand out of the prayer position, and I was able to put my finger under it. I pressed it and the door burst open. I couldn't believe it!

I scrambled out of the locker, relieved and empowered. I felt I could do anything. I was glad to be free, of course, but something much larger and consequential happened that day. I was more elated that I had just discovered how to relate directly to God.

I also realized, for the first time, that I was truly alone in this world. I was a separate human entity from everyone and everything. There was no one there to ask for help. Not my parents, or my brother or anyone else in the entire world. I only had me. I was alone, yet God was there to guide and protect me. This thought anchored in me. Going forward, I'd make decisions and take action with God always there to provide me with guidance and love.

This childhood moment was the foundation for my lifelong one-on-one relationship with God. Even though my family attended the Lutheran church every week, and I went to Sunday school, this was its own thing. Somehow I knew, even at that young age, that this was bigger. This one experience made all of those gatherings meaningless because they had nothing to do with my personal communication with God.

The power is not in the weekly gatherings; the magic is created by connecting one-on-one with the source that is within. You had to take the time to sit quietly and listen. Once I burst out of the constraints of that locked metal door, I knew that I was powerful, that I could conquer anything as long as I stayed connected with the pureness of the creator of life.

When my mom picked me up, she asked why I had bruises on my leg. I looked down and saw black and blue marks from my mid-thigh to my ankle, on both the inside and outside of my right leg. I told her I bruised it in the pool. I still don't know why I lied to her. Maybe I wasn't ready to tell her what had happened. Maybe it felt too enormous to put into words. Most likely, I didn't think she'd understand what had happened—even *I* barely understood. But I would learn.

From that day forward I felt I had a secret. I finally understood why the minister at our church would say, "You should love no one above God." Before the locker incident, I sincerely loved my mom more than God. My mom was always there for me. She loved me and took good care of my every need and concern. When I found myself in that locker, I realized that my mom couldn't help me—she would have if she had known, but she didn't. But God *was there*. I started to read the Bible every evening before bed. I'd flip through the pages, stop and put my finger on a verse. It never failed to be a meaningful message. I was convinced that each and every night God was showing me what I needed to see.

I've since grown in my understanding of what God means to me, especially in the last ten years. I've come to feel comfortable referring to God as "Universe" or "Source Energy" or even "All That Is." I certainly don't claim to have all the answers, but as I've expanded, so has my definition of what I call God. However, I do know that, whatever I call It, It has been with me for every breath that I have drawn in my life.

****

After being in Minnesota for a year, our family returned to Colorado just as I was going into the second grade. We lived in a remote area west of Denver in the foothills of the Rocky Mountains. At night, as I lay in bed, I'd hear my parents arguing in their bedroom. One night I heard the loud thump of my father throwing a book against the wall. I jumped out of bed and ran into their room.

"I don't want you to get a divorce!" I screamed.

"Go back to bed!" roared my dad.

I did what he said. Then I prayed: *Dear God, please don't let my parents get divorced.*

I began to have really disturbing thoughts, especially for a young girl. I saw shadows of cowboys and Indians fighting outside my windows. I was afraid that someone would pour poison in my mouth if I slept with it open. If my feet weren't tucked up underneath me, I feared there was real a chance that an intruder would chop my feet off with an ax.

Dear God, please keep me safe tonight. I don't want to die in my sleep.

As beautiful as it was to live in the shadow of the Rockies, the conditions were not easy. We were always short on water. Bathing required using one tub for multiple consecutive occupants. We occasionally had to take our laundry into Denver when there was a chance that our well would run dry. In the winter, the quarter-mile dirt road that led to our house was frequently buried deep with snow. Occasionally when we left the house to get groceries, we would have to use a sled to schlep our supplies and bags of groceries up the steep driveway. It was tough, but I had other things that a young girl would only dream of, like two ponies and a horse.

When I was nine, my dad, my brother Eric and I were in the yellow pickup on Interstate 285, a two-lane highway that connected Denver to the heart of the mountains. Dad pulled the truck over onto the wide shoulder and turned off the engine. I was sitting in the middle of the bench seat. Cars sailed by on our left.

"I wanted to tell you that your mother and I don't love each other anymore," he said. "After today, I won't be living at the house. We're getting a divorce."

I looked at my hands. I used the thumbnail on my right hand to split the layers of my thumbnail on my left.

"I'll be moving into an apartment in Denver, and the two of you can visit me every other weekend."

I started shredding the nail on my left index finger.

"Come on, guys. Say something. This isn't easy for me," he said. "Lisa, stop doing that. Look at me."

I looked up at him and started to cry. "I don't want you to leave, Daddy."

It didn't matter. We drove home and he packed his bags and left. My mom sat crying on the couch.

"It's okay, Mom. It'll be okay." I hugged her to make it better.

At night I would pray in my room: *Dear God, my parents are getting a divorce. Where are you? How could you let this happen? Please help us!* I thought God would always answer my prayers, but this time He didn't.

Going to church pretty much ended as a family activity once my father was no longer in the house. Occasionally, my mom would take me to the local community church. I really enjoyed it and would feel guilty when I couldn't go.

My mom remarried about three years after the divorce. Her new husband, Gary, had been a Lutheran minister, but he was interested in going back to school to get into television work. We all moved so Gary could attend the University of Wisconsin. After one year we moved to Minnetonka, Minnesota, where our family became involved with the Lutheran church there. Even though Gary was no longer a practicing minister, he still felt it was important for all of us to attend church weekly.

I became a youth leader along with my friend Joy, who was a year ahead of me in school. Joy and I ran our youth group, helping to organize our events and gatherings. The youth minister, Pastor Paul, was really the driving force of our group. In his late thirties, boyish looking and dynamic, he was married with two adorable children that he and his wife had adopted. Pastor Paul was always coming up with ways we could spread the gospel. One of the most fun ideas was "Clowning for Christ." We'd dress up in clown outfits and act out the weekly gospel during the church service.

The fifteen members would break a parable down into small parts to act them out. We all wore outlandish costumes. I had an electric-orange Afro wig, with an orange-and-blue clown suit that my mother had made for me for Halloween years earlier. My face was painted white with comically large red lips, a red foam clown nose, and a giant blue tear beneath my right eye. One of the parables we performed was the Prodigal Son. I adored playing the bad son who was forgiven when he returned to his father.

In 1983, the youth group took a bus trip from Minnesota to San Antonio, Texas, for the Lutheran Youth Convention. Pastor Paul rented an additional hotel room so we could use it as the meeting place for our Bible studies and team building. It was a life-changing experience and opened my eyes to a lot of things—not all of them good. For one, I noticed that every time a group of us was out exploring the city, Joy would never be with us.

At one point I blurted out, "Oh, she and Paul are up in that extra room doing it!" I was just making a joke for the rest of the group.

The following summer before I went to college, I had mentioned to Joy that while we were in San Antonio several of us joked that she and Paul had been having sex in the extra room at the convention. Her eyes got big.

"What? Why would you think that?"

"Oh, we were just making up stories when you weren't there," I said.

"I can't believe you guys would even joke about that!" she said.

A few months later, during my first semester at college, I received a hysterical call from my mother.

"Lisa, did he touch you? Oh, my goodness, I just found out! Did Pastor Paul touch you?"

"Mom, what are you talking about?"

"Pastor Paul! He just admitted to having sex with some girls in your confirmation class!"

I was floored. In fact, that doesn't even cover it. "What? No he did not! What are you talking about?"

"He just resigned from the church. He admitted to having sex with girls from our church, and from the last church he was at too. Apparently, one of the girls from his old church was in a psychology class, and they started talking about how people in authority, like pastors, can take advantage of those who need their help. Did he touch you?"

"Mom, no. Of course he didn't touch me. This is just someone making up stories. I don't believe it. Paul taught me everything about God and Jesus—he couldn't have done this. I don't believe you!"

I started to panic. It couldn't be true.

"Sweetheart, I know," my mom continued. "This is a lot to take in. I just wanted to be sure that he hadn't done anything to you. Sit with this for a while and let's talk again later. It'll be okay. I love you so much."

It turned out that he *was* having sex with Joy in that extra rented room in San Antonio. When I'd blurted that out during our trip, it seemed so over the top—my conscious self didn't believe it was possible—but Spirit knew. And Spirit was using me to get the message out.

Incredibly, Paul's previous church leaders *knew* about his behavior and decided to quietly move him to our church. His wife knew too.

I can't overestimate how much this shattered my world, which was already fragile to begin with. Paul had been an anchor to something that I was giving my life to and he had betrayed it, me, and the whole youth group.

How could I believe in anything that he had taught me? He had desecrated every teaching and lesson that he shared with us. After the news finally sunk in, I was able to look back and see how he had been trying to worm his way into my life: The hug that lasted too long, the fingers that brushed against my breasts as he put his arm around my waist. There was the time he invited me into the church basement and the lights were off, and he shared with me how he wanted his daughter to grow up to be just like me.

I remember that during touch football, he would be way too rough with my good friends Tim and Dave. He would literally take them out, tackling them so hard they had bumps and bruises, especially after they had dared to spend time with one of "his" girls. It was unnerving to look back at the past events in this new light; there were so many instances that were so wrong. At the time, I just couldn't put all the pieces together. Probably, I didn't want to. When we are young, we latch on to truths so tightly that it's dangerous to consider how unsteady they truly are.

The whole thing was heartbreaking. Joy moved to Great Britain as soon as the news came out. I never had the chance to discuss any of this with her. While we were friends, I knew that she had been having issues with her parents and had turned to Pastor Paul for help. This made the whole situation even worse.

Between the Pastor Paul incident and soon after discovering that my mother's husband Gary, who had returned to working for the Lutheran church, was having an affair with his secretary, I gave up organized religion.

I decided that if Pastor Paul and my stepfather, who had taught me about God and religion, were filled with sin, then their teachings must be false. I questioned the reality of God and everything that I had been taught. My personal connection with God had vanished. *How could I have been so betrayed?*

****

A few years later, incident after incident would occur that would rattle my world, transform it, and bring me headlong back to my faith. I moved to San Francisco after graduating in 1989. Ian and I met and started dating the day after the World Series earthquake.

Two years later, on the day we got engaged, a fire destroyed over three thousand homes around Oakland. Ian lived there and his house narrowly survived—all the houses on the other side of the street had burned down. I wondered if God was trying to get my attention.

That same weekend, I received a call from the adoption agency that had placed me as baby. My birth mother wanted to meet me. There was so much going on. I couldn't deal with meeting her or even talking to her at that point. Maybe I just wasn't ready for it at all.

My life began to feel out of control, and even though I was not at all interested in organized religion, I felt a deep need to be married in a church—it didn't matter which one. The local Episcopalian church was available on the same day that we were able to book the reception site. My uncle from Vermont was an Episcopalian minister and agreed to perform the ceremony for us.

Two weeks after we married, we moved to Washington D.C. for Ian's job. His father came to visit over Labor Day. We had a nice evening meal and conversation; the next morning Ian's father dropped dead of a heart attack. The event was shocking and threw my equilibrium off so much that I felt an urgent need to re-connect with God.

Seven months later, I happily discovered I was pregnant with Jenna. I suddenly wanted to find out as much as I could about my birth parents. I realized that because of my adoption, I didn't know the basic facts about my genetic health and how this could potentially affect my baby. I wrote a letter to my birth mother, Debbie, asking her all sorts of questions, which she answered.

Unfortunately, all the medical information in the world couldn't prepare us for the birth of our daughter. Jenna was born with a birth defect—her esophagus wasn't attached to her stomach; it was attached to her lungs. She also had a blockage in her lower stomach. If the doctors hadn't realized this, we would have unknowingly fed her, causing her to aspirate and die.

A new neonatologist was on call at the local hospital the night Jenna was born. He'd recently finished a rotation at Children's Hospital, in Washington D.C.

Fortunately he was very familiar with Jenna's problem. I've always felt that God had put him there that night to save Jenna's life. She was immediately transported to Children's and underwent six hours of surgery. My faith was back; I began praying every minute of every day. You don't realize how much you love something until you think you might lose it.

I asked Ian's father, in heaven, to watch over her and keep her safe. The doctors told us that Jenna would need to be in the hospital for three months, but she went home after two weeks. They called her the "miracle baby." God had answered my prayers.

Four months after Jenna was born, I flew to Denver to meet my birth mother. I was very emotional during the trip. I knew that I needed God's help. I already had a mother, the woman who raised me; I didn't want or need another one. I began having second thoughts about meeting my birth mother at all. Maybe it was important to me in the past, but at that point, I wasn't so sure.

We met at the Lutheran Service Society. My mom had agreed to go with Jenna and me. Ian didn't want any part of it because of his resentment about his own birth mother's decision to give him away.

At the adoption center, we were led to a small room. They brought in Debbie and her oldest daughter Kristen, my nineteen-year-old half-sister. Seeing my birth mother floored me. I looked absolutely nothing like her. I had pictured this meeting a thousand times, but the reality was nothing like my imagination. There were awkward hugs and lots of tears.

It was obvious that my half-sister was pregnant. She explained that she had dropped out of school. It made me wonder what my life would have been like if I hadn't been given up for adoption. For me, up to this point in my life, I always had positive feelings about being adopted. I thought my adoption was just part of God's plan.

After chatting for a while, we discovered that Debbie's grandfather and my adopted grandfather, incredibly, knew each other as young men. They had both grown up and lived in a tiny town in Essex, Iowa (pop. 763). Later, we found a photograph of the two of them when they were on the same football team in high school. I was amazed that even though I was born in Denver, our families had intersected sixty years earlier in a tiny town in Iowa. Again, I felt that God has designed a grand plan; as far as I was concerned, there were simply no coincidences.

****

In the spring of 1996, when Jenna was one and a half and Robert was six months old, Ian and I moved to Ridgefield, Connecticut. When we first drove through Ridgefield, I spotted a beautiful stone church on Main Street, an Episcopal church named St. Stephen's. I took it as a sign— this was the same name and denomination of the church that Ian and I were married in out in California. I told him that I could see Jenna getting married in that church one day. Soon after we moved into our house, right in the heart of town, I walked over to St. Stephen's and stumbled upon their once-a-year outdoor service. I wasn't dressed to sit on the grass and a very kind woman offered a corner of her blanket for me to sit on. I immediately felt at home at this church.

As Jenna and Robbie were getting older, like a lot of parents, I felt the weight of the responsibility for their spiritual education. It was up to me to get involved, and I did. I volunteered to teach Sunday school, and joined the Youth Advisory Board. I made friends with Lisa and Susie who both had boys in the threes program with Jenna. The weekly church services gave me comfort. I was a stay-at-home mother, and it was a great outlet to interact with other people and to reconnect with my religious upbringing.

It was a year later, spring of 1997, that everything came crashing to a halt and time stood still. It started with something so basic; a doctor's visit for me and then a couple of days later one for Ian.

I discovered a spot on my back that was very painful, like someone was sticking a needle into my skin. Ian looked at it and said it was nothing. I woke up a day later with an enlarged lymph node on my neck. I called the doctor and scheduled an appointment. I was diagnosed with shingles, a dreadfully painful disease that, if not treated, can go on for months as an agonizing rash.

I called Ian at work, almost gloating that he'd been wrong. "Ha, I really have something, and it requires medication."

"Well, I have a swollen lymph node on my neck, too," he said.

"You'd better get to the doctor right away."
Stress can bring on shingles. I worried Ian had it because he'd worked sixty straight days without time off—he was a tax attorney, and it was the busy season. He made the appointment and went in two days later on a Sunday.

That same weekend, coincidentally, my mother had flown in for a quick weekend visit. Little did I know when she arrived what a blessing it was to have her there.

Ian walked out of the doctor's office with a slip of paper.

I figured he'd been given the same diagnosis I had, so I said, "Let's go to the pharmacy and get your prescription filled."

Ian looked like he had been hit by a truck.

"It's not a prescription; it's for a CAT scan. The doctor thinks I have cancer."

"What?" I was dumbfounded, too shocked to take in what he was saying.

My mom stayed with the children while Ian and I went directly to the hospital for what we didn't know would be the first of many CAT scans. Two weeks later he was diagnosed with Hodgkin's lymphoma. We were told that this was "very treatable" and with six months of chemotherapy he'd be in the clear. This was not the case. On Christmas Eve 1997, more tests revealed non-Hodgkin's lymphoma in his system, which would require more intensive treatments and a much worse prognosis.

Throughout my life, I have found that things always happen for a reason. I was convinced that my shingles brought Ian to the doctor. I was also convinced that the Universe knew that we needed my mother's help.

At the time, I was seeing a massage therapist as I had struggled with back pain for many years. I told the therapist, Alice, that my husband had been diagnosed with cancer. She was sympathetic and nurturing. Then she started to talk to me about angels.

At first, I was skeptical. I was raised to believe in God and God alone. As I continued to go to see her, she educated me on how she would ask the angels for anything and everything, even something as simple as a parking place. Alice would tell me all sorts of stories about the amazing things that would happen when she would request things from her angels. She also introduced me to Reiki, an energy healing modality. I decided to get the first level of training with her, as I hoped to learn the technique and use it on Ian.

After a full year of cancer treatments, including a stem-cell transplant at Sloan Kettering Hospital in New York City, Ian went into remission. Even though Ian had been sick, his company, General Electric, continued to promote him. We were moved to Ohio for nine months and then to New Jersey. This was quite an accomplishment considering the whirlwind situation he was going through.

With the stress of Ian's illness and all the relocations, I was in agony with my back and thought maybe surgery would be the answer. However, a physical therapist warned me that some patients actually got worse after an operation. Not being able to find *someone* or *something* to fix my problem left me feeling hopeless and frustrated. Soon after that warning, I was watching a news program with John Stossel of ABC's 20/20. I dozed off. Suddenly near the end of the show I woke up. John had started to discuss the book *Mind Over Back Pain,* by John Sarno, a medical doctor at the New York Medical Center. Stossel explained how this book had saved his life from debilitating back pain. I bought the book the very next day.

Sarno argued that if you were to X-ray everyone's back, chances were there would be some sort of medically diagnosable issue. If you were prone to internalize stress then the stress showed up in this weak link and created pain. Once a person heard that they had a "problem," his or her mind began to support the "problem" and might even create more of a "problem" to justify how they were feeling. Then when several doctors agreed that this "problem" needed medical intervention, he or she felt validated. But if a person chose *not* to buy into the "problem" and allowed the stress to dissipate, the back pain went away. This was radically new thinking for me, but I gave it a try, and it changed my life. Within three months my pain began to diminish. After a year, I had zero back pain. Absolutely none. I had found the answer, and all along it was within me.

This book woke me up to something essential, something that would become such a key part of my understanding about life and healing: The truth of the body-mind connection. Up until this point in my life, I had no idea that you could control so much with your brain. I also learned some ways to alleviate my stress with mantras and meditation. A whole new world started to open up for me.

****

It was around our tenth anniversary, in 2002, that Ian began to have night sweats and chills. I begged him to go to the doctor and get tested, but he refused. I threatened to take the kids away, but he still wouldn't go. It was only when he was interested in a job in Seattle that he agreed to go in for a check up to prove me wrong. The minute the doctor told us the lymphoma was back, I knew intuitively that he wasn't going to make it. I saw my life shift before my eyes. And I had to carry the burden of knowing it.

My friend Lisa was going through the same thing at the same time. Her husband, Stan, the golf pro, had been diagnosed with tongue cancer. Lisa and I started to get together once a week to have breakfast and talk. One morning, she suggested that we walk down the block to Touch of Sedona, a spiritual boutique. She said she'd gone to a few angel-reading sessions and found them to be helpful. I was both skeptical and curious, so I agreed to go.

When we arrived, we were greeted by the smell of wild and exotic incense. The owner of the store welcomed us and told us that Penny would do a free fifteen minute angel-reading for each of us. Lisa went first; she disappeared behind a closed door in the back of the store. I wandered around looking at all the Indian and wolf paintings on the walls and thumbed through the books on crystals, healings, meditation, and tarot. I hadn't realized how complex and intricate this world was, how deep it went. There were all sorts of categories I wasn't very familiar with. It was an eye-opening experience.

When it was my turn, I walked to the back of the store. Penny greeted me and showed me where to sit. The room was small with just enough room for a card table and a chair on each side. She asked my name and took out a stack of cards, shuffled them and put them face up on the table. There was some angelic music softly playing. Penny started to read the cards.

She said that the angels wanted to let me know that they were with me during this difficult time. I started to cry. She said my angels were always with me and that if I needed anything to just ask them for their help. I can't remember if Penny asked me more questions or what exactly she told me, but I remembered feeling both overwhelmed and reassured at the same time. I left the store with an angel CD and the book *Angelspeake: How to Talk with Your Angels*, by Barbara Mark and Trudy Griswold.

The book's directions were simple. You cleared your mind, prayed to your angels, and then you began to write what you heard inside your head. The first time I did it, I was hooked. I wrote that my angels loved me, that they were surrounding me at all times, and the more I talked to them, the more easily the readings would become. Here's one of my first angel self-readings:

Your life has meaning for others. You just have to present the material in such a way that people find it useful and inspiring. You are off to a great start. Keep writing and keep thinking. Your message will be loud and clear, you just need to hone your skills to be able to share the information that is most important to other people. We are here to help you and to guide you—don't get frustrated or discouraged. This is a path that you will continue to follow for the rest of your life. It's not a race; it's a journey. Know that we are always here and always with you. Just continue to write and again, your message will come through.

Love and blessings, your Angels

I continued channeling the angels, who were so helpful during this very stressful time. I also reached out to my priest at St. Stephen's. The rector, or main priest, was going on vacation and suggested that I meet with Daryl, the new assistant priest. I called Daryl, and he suggested that I pick him up at the church and that we go out for lunch, ideally out of town, so we wouldn't be interrupted by anyone from the church while we chatted.

Apparently he and his wife shared a car, so he walked to work each day. I picked him up at the church in my minivan. He was a handsome man in his mid-thirties, just over six feet tall, with tussled dark brown hair and a boyish smile. I didn't know why, but I felt nervous. Pretty soon, I would learn that my intuition was correct.

We arrived at the restaurant in the next town. The waiter asked for our drink order.

"We'll have a bottle of the house Chardonnay," he said without hesitation.

I was stunned. Did he think we were on a date?

He told stories about his drug-crazed college days, and then shifted into how a person should raise their children—he had two—and discussed the role of a good wife.

Being the polite Midwestern girl that I was, I sat in a state of shock. *Could I really be sitting here with the minister of my church drinking wine and hearing these intimate details of his life?*

Honestly, I was somewhat intrigued but mostly horrified. This was supposed to be a comfort to me. It wasn't. Not once did he ask about Ian or our situation, which was ostensibly the whole point of getting together.

By the end of lunch, I was getting annoyed and wanted to get out of there. When I dropped him back at the church, I thanked him for his time. He turned, looked at me, hesitated and then leaned forward and kissed me, full on the lips. I was disgusted and pulled back in shock. He got out of the car. I wiped my lips with my sleeve. I was in shock. What had just happened?

Though it wasn't as drastic, this was like a replay of the whole Pastor Paul situation from my youth. I was appalled by the way Daryl had handled my "counseling session," and I discussed the situation with the main minister. He told me I must have misunderstood and that I was overreacting. I now had a better understanding of how my friends were preyed upon by the youth minister so many years ago. Some people in positions of influence have no shame—they take advantage of their status and of others' belief in them. It was repulsive.

As a member of the church, I was taught to look up to my pastors, as they were the authorities. I originally felt honored by the special attention when the minister took me to lunch. In reality it was a way for him to use his power over me, which was especially egregious considering I was in such a vulnerable situation. My husband was dying; I was looking for spiritual support, not a glass of wine!

I was dissatisfied as well with the rector's handling of the event. He suggested I talk to Daryl and explain how I was feeling, saying, "I'm sure he can straighten out the situation." This was a terrible idea. I had absolutely no interest in speaking with Daryl again.

Several months went by and I ultimately reported Daryl to the Connecticut State Dioceses. An investigation ensued. Daryl was reprimanded. He was eventually let go from our church. Based on rumors it was not because of the way he treated me (and another woman who complained about his behavior), but due to discrepancies with his expense forms. Incredible. The whole incident distanced me, once again, from organized religion. My trust had been violated. I was sensing a pattern.

The night Ian died and I dreamed of heaven, my spiritual life utterly changed. Being given the opportunity to view the place that Ian was stepping into gave me such peace and comfort. Even if this representation wasn't the actual "heaven," I felt that God revealed to me a place that would make sense to me and allow me to know that Ian would be fine. I had been worried that Ian wasn't baptized and yet God showed me that he would not only be fine, but was welcomed with open arms.

The rules of my organized religion began to melt away when I realized that they didn't matter at all. It struck me that every rule that was taught to me was a *man-made* rule, not God's rule. I also felt like if I had been brought up with a different religion then I would have been shown their idea of what heaven is. If everyone had their own, then none could be the "right" one.

God, Universe, Source Energy—whatever you call "All that Is"—just wants us to feel the love It has for us and for us to love one another and be happy. Even though losing Ian was difficult, seeing where he would be going allowed me to feel the love that constantly surrounds us. The gift I received that night allowed me to know that it doesn't matter what anyone else does or says; the only thing that matters is that once I connected to "All that Is," my spiritual life, my work life, my whole life, was never the same—it would forever be filled with the love from Spirit.

CHAPTER 6

December 2004

A fter returning home from Denver that first holiday season with David, he asked me to go to a jewelry store. He wanted to know what type of diamond I liked. I was excited, of course, but also caught off-guard. We went, and I tried on rings with different-shaped diamonds and decided I liked the square ones the best. Afterwards, nothing was mentioned again. I didn't quite know what to make of this excursion.

Three weeks later we all flew to Ireland so the kids and I could meet David's mom, brothers and sisters. David flew out a week earlier so he could attend a small memorial service for the one-year anniversary of his father's death, which interestingly was the same day as my brother's birthday, January 15th.

The kids had never been to Europe, so it was a real adventure. We arrived in Dublin at 6 a.m., and David was in the terminal waiting for us. He drove us to his sister Esme's house in Dalkey, just outside of the city. We met her five children. Kerrie was the oldest, then Lucie, Sophie and Emilie, who were all around the same age as Jenna.

The youngest, Jack, who was three, was excited to have Robbie there to tackle and play games with, especially coming from a household of all women.

The next day we drove down to David's mum's home in the country. She had the same smiling blue eyes as her son and stood just four feet eleven inches. Given her petite stature, I couldn't imagine that she had given birth to seven children! Her lilting Irish accent was rhythmic and soothing. As a former Montessori teacher, she was extremely welcoming and instructive on many subjects, as well as very direct. She took no time just going head-on with what was on her mind.

"So Lisa, are you dating David just to have help with the children?"

Whoa.

I was prepared for direct, but this was completely unexpected. Feeling as though I had been knocked off my feet, I stammered out an answer, "No. No, of course not. I'm dating David because he's a wonderful man and I..."

"Well, I'm sure it must be difficult. I see how my daughter struggles without her husband. I would just hope that there is more to your relationship than just someone to help you out." Her mother bear qualities were showing.

I couldn't quite figure out how to respond.

She continued with a twinkle in her eye, "I'd like you to know that David has *never* brought a girlfriend home before. I would say that he is quite taken with you."

My heart soared. I took this as proof that David was even more serious than I had thought. I remembered our trip to the jewelry store and thought that he might propose while we were in Ireland.

Every time we went anywhere for the next several days, I braced myself for the big proposal. By the last night, I had run out of patience. We went out to dinner with his family to a picturesque restaurant. I thought, *Okay this is it.* The dinner came and went and still nothing.

On the way out of the restaurant, I went into the ladies' room, feeling desperate and disappointed. I looked at each of the three stalls and each stall had a locking device that when the stall was occupied read, "Engaged."

I freaked. The Universe was working against me. I stormed out and ran directly into David.

"What's wrong?" David asked.

"What's wrong? Even the fucking bathroom stalls are engaged!" I was enraged, just not myself at all.

"What?" David started to chuckle.

"I thought you were going to propose to me here, David. In Ireland. Every time we went to a place with a beautiful view, or went out for a big family dinner, I thought you were going to propose. Why did you take me to look at rings?"

David hugged me. "Oh baby, I'm sorry you're disappointed. I was never planning on proposing while we were here. I feel like out of respect, for you and for Ian, I should wait until after the year anniversary of his death."

I was touched and yet let down. The fact that he didn't want to do anything to disrespect Ian was admirable, but I have to admit that I didn't like the idea that we were doing anything wrong. I knew we weren't; we were in love. We hadn't planned it, and we certainly weren't disrespecting anyone. I didn't care what the society police thought. Hadn't I been through enough?

****

With Ian's death, my newfound spiritual outlook on life and the whirlwind romance with David, my life was completely upended. Many of the beliefs that I had grown up with had fallen away; many more weren't making sense to me any longer. At one point I remember telling David that I was scared that I was so happy. He didn't understand this at all; how could I have trepidation about *positive* feelings? I explained to him that I was at the top of my "happiness meter" and that if any more goodness came into my life, I feared something bad would happen. He gently laughed and pulled me close. "Sweetheart, there's no limit to happiness," he said.

At that moment my imagined glass ceiling of happiness just shattered. For the first time in my life I felt that I could take a deep breath and actually embrace the joy in my heart. It was ironic; even though my life had been turned *upside down,* for the first time I was actually seeing the world the way I *was supposed to see it.* To me, everything was right side up.

Three days after the one-year anniversary of Ian's death, David proposed. He did so on bended knee with a gorgeous three-stone, square-cut diamond ring.

"The big one in the middle is for you, and the two smaller ones on each side are for Jenna and Robbie. Not only do I want to be your husband, I want to be their dad."

He had me since the bar stool at Upstream. Of course, I said yes.

Simultaneously, the lease on David's apartment was up. He graciously moved in with us. Into the house that I had owned and lived in with my first husband, the house where ultimately Ian had died. Living somewhere else hadn't even crossed my mind. In retrospect, I'm surprised that David was okay with this—as I don't know if I would have been okay with the situation if our roles were reversed.

We spent the next year making plans for our destination wedding. A year to the day after David proposed we were married at the One and Only Ocean Club in the Bahamas, surrounded by seventy-five of our friends and family. The weather was perfect and as an added excitement, *Casino Royale*, the James Bond movie, was being filmed on property as we were saying our vows.

Over the next several months, we turned our attention to making the house into a home that was more our own. We decided to renovate and made a list of items we wanted to change: Adding a third bay to the garage, creating a room above it so the kids could have a playroom; replacing the kitchen countertops with granite; installing a wine fridge; and redoing the master bath. We also wanted to buy an extra refrigerator for the garage. We hired an architect and submitted forms for approval for a three-foot variance. We were told that we should be ready to break ground within four to six weeks.

Everything that could go wrong did. First the architect filed the wrong paper work—a four-week delay. Then the town lost our paper work, an additional six-week delay. We were finally scheduled for the Planning and Zoning meeting for the month of June, but the required newspaper notice went missing, so we were pushed to July. At the July meeting, there wasn't a quorum, so the meeting was adjourned, and the month of August was a vacation month. Then a board member came to our house to look at the staked out three-foot variance, but at the meeting he couldn't remember what it looked like; another month delay. After nearly nine months, our variance was finally approved.

The week of the approval, as I drove by a beautiful lake home that had been on the market for six months, I noticed that a new real estate company was representing the house. I had driven by this house on a regular basis as it was on the route to Jenna's school—and I'd always been drawn to it on a gut level. The people living there had been renovating the house for almost two years.

During the early stages of their construction, I had called my real estate friend, Lee, to see if she knew if they were fixing up the house to be sold.

"No. They're just fixing it up for themselves."

"Too bad. I could see myself living there one day."

As it turned out, as soon as the couple was done with the renovations, Lee called to tell me that the husband had been transferred to Texas for a new job, and that they were listing the property for sale. At that time, however, the house was way beyond our budget.

The day I saw the new real estate sign I called Lee, after dropping Jenna at school, and asked her why they had changed agents.

"Hmm, let me see. Oh my goodness, it's gone to a relo company. The price dropped yesterday, by quite a bit! It looks like the owners must have taken a buyout, and the relocation company wants to sell it as soon as possible to get it off their books. Do you want to see it?"

"Yes!"

I called David at work. The three of us walked in the front door, turned and looked out the two-story glass windows at a stunning lake view. We hadn't even taken a step out of the main room and I said, "We'll take it!"

The house came about because of a lot of different spiritual connections. I would've seen them as coincidences when I was younger, but by this point I saw what they really were. For one, Lee kept saying how the house reminded her of a "Colorado house." She was right; the architecture was similar to a ski lodge and after growing up in Colorado and spending a lot of time in ski lodges, it *felt* like home. The entire front of the house was filled with windows and on the inside there were large wood beams. A fireplace went from the floor to the second story ceiling and an open staircase led to the second floor bedrooms. Also, the address of the home was the same numbers as my Colorado area code when I was growing up.

All items on our list for renovating our current house were already in the new house, including the extra fridge in the garage! In my heart, I suddenly realized that all of the absurd delays for the approval of the variance had been divinely directed, Spirit's way of delaying us so we'd end up in the perfect house at the exact right time. We actually moved in on my fortieth birthday! At the beginning of the year I had asked the angels to give me something special for my birthday, and that it didn't matter what it was, but I wanted it to be something amazing. It was, and the fact that it was also on a lake was icing on the cake. You simply can't make this stuff up!

Moving had another tremendous advantage. As a new family, this was the best thing we could have done. I hadn't realized how much baggage was attached to the home where Ian had died. Robbie was terrified to be alone there, not wanting to be there unless someone was with him. The energy in that home was heavy and sad.

I realized this only after we moved and felt the amazing freedom, clarity and optimism radiating from the core of our new home. The move was critical for us; we had to start together in a new place, as a family. Once we did it, it seemed so obvious how much we needed it.

I decided to hire someone to help move the energy in the old house so we could sell it. I went to Touch of Sedona for a recommendation. I was led to Carol, who called herself a "space clearer." When she came into our old house, I led her around and filled her in on the six years we'd lived there, including Ian's death. It was incredible; she was able to tell me things that there was no way she could have known.

In the kitchen, she pointed out the window. "Ian's telling me this is where he liked to sit and watch the birds." The feeder was no longer there; there was simply no way on earth she could have known this. It seemed clear to me—as someone who intimately knew that house—that she was channeling my dead husband.

We went upstairs to the master bedroom. Now, to be clear, there was *no furniture* in the entire house. As we walked into the room, she immediately stopped and aimed the palm of her hand in the spot where our bed used to be.

"I feel stuck energy right here," she said.

"Oh my God, that's where Ian died."

I started crying. She asked me to kneel on the floor.

"I see an angel right behind you. I'm going to ask her to wrap her wings around you," she said. "Let's ask for this stuck energy to move into the next dimension for the highest and greatest good for all, so this room is cleared of heavy energy."

We walked into the guest room. She continued, "Okay, I see a family that's going to move in here. They're going to use this room as a child's room. The family has three children, two boys and a girl. They're on their way."

Two months later, a family with that exact makeup purchased the home.

It was another confirmation that a direct connection to Spirit was so much more helpful to everyday life than organized religion had ever been for me. It was so much more comfortable to be around people like Carol than it was to be around a structured, regulated notion of what a connection to God was "dictated" to be.

After we moved into the new house, I felt a slight shift toward resentment from a few friends. It was almost like they were jealous or angry that I had found not only a new husband, but also a new house.

I've never been able to put my finger on exactly what the issue was. I had felt this invisible resentment throughout my life. In high school, some unknown people took shaving cream and scrawled *slut, bitch,* and *whore* across the front of the garage doors at my house. My dorm room door in college would have similar sentiments written on it one time. To this day, I'm unclear as to why people feel it's necessary to take someone down when they see he or she is happy. Once it became clear that some of my old friends were feeling negative about this phase in my life, I decided I couldn't let it grow and spread.

I had one friend in particular who was very supportive during Ian's illness and especially after his death. However, once I began dating David and spending more time with him, she tried to undermine my relationship, saying things like, "Don't you know that all golf pros sleep with the women that they give lessons to?" And when she learned that he was thirty-nine and never married, she snidely stated that he must have a fear of commitment.

She would also make other smug or condescending comments, like how the heart-shaped box of chocolates David bought me for Valentine's Day was "lowbrow." It reached a point where I couldn't accept it anymore. Her negativity felt like an assault. I wrote her a letter:

Dear _____,

As much as I value our friendship, my life is going in a new direction. Although I know you have concerns about my new relationship, I need to follow my heart and see what is going to happen. Please know that this is not about you, but about me growing and needing to be free to explore and experience this next part of my life. Therefore I would like to request that you no longer call or contact me. I know that we live in the same community, and would hope that we can see one another in social situations without creating a scene or making this a bigger deal than it is—that we are both moving forward on our own.

I have to give her credit; after she received the letter we never discussed it, and when we ran into one another, we'd say a polite hello and move on.

There were other friends who only found time for me when I was helping or listening to them—just one-way friendships that, after David came into my life, I wouldn't tolerate anymore. With my spiritual awakening, it was no longer who I was. While Ian was sick, I was so needy that I gave everything away—but now that I was feeling good about myself, I just couldn't do it anymore.

I later found out that losing friends was often a necessary part and condition of spiritual growth as we leave behind old paradigms and make space for new ones. Though it was necessary—and healthy—it was still painful. We must shed the old, the comfortable, the familiar, in order to step forward into what we really need and what we've always wanted.

****

The next year I found myself nesting in our new home and enjoying the newfound happiness of being married and living as a normal family—something I hadn't had for a long time. Before we were married, David and I discussed his desire to adopt my children, so we could legally be a family unit. We contacted an attorney and made all of the necessary arrangements. I found it serendipitous that my mom and dad had adopted me, and Ian's mom had adopted him, and now David would be adopting Ian's and my children. I struggled with what to do with their last names; in fact, I agonized over it. This was their identity, Ian's identity—their view of themselves and how the world would view them. *Was it my right to change that?* Then something David said crystallized my view.

"I am so thankful that Ian was their father for seven and nine years. He gave them life. But going forward, I hope to be their dad for at least forty to fifty years. I would like them to have my name."

I decided that instead of losing anything, we were

all gaining something. That was it; we made it official. We all got a new name and added it to our previous names. After some initial confusion with the new names at school—like having to change home rooms to sit with the J last names, rather than the S last names—the kids eventually settled into their new identities.

During the latter half of the year, I began to feel I needed to get more seriously back into the workforce. I had been a stay-at-home mom for thirteen years, as well as a caregiver to Ian for several years. A few times I had attempted to start a new career path, like when I created Breast Pumps Express, my own business where I rented breast pumps to new mothers. Then there was the real estate thing that I quit after six months. And of course the acting, which was fun, but was too unpredictable and didn't allow me to be me. I didn't know exactly what I wanted to do, but I figured the best paying job I could get would be back in the accounting world. I decided that my ideal job would be a part-time accounting position at a hedge fund, as they were the most generous in their pay. I also wanted to work in town, so I wouldn't have to deal with a long commute. I half-heartedly put it out to the Universe and waited—meaning I sent my résumé to a couple of headhunter firms, but did nothing more than that.

Meanwhile, I flew to Minnesota to visit my mom and to spend some time with one of my closest high school friends. She had been a huge support during Ian's illness and after his death. We never spent much time together, but she was always there for me, especially on my once-a-year visits back to Minnesota where she took time to meet and just talk. Her husband, also an old friend of mine, had sadly committed suicide just before Thanksgiving, leaving her with five young boys. The situation was heartbreaking.

I was floored when I had received the news from her mom. How could this have happened? Wrapping my mind around someone who dies from cancer was hard enough. But I struggled with understanding how someone could decide to take their own life, especially when Ian tried so hard to stay alive. I obviously don't know the internal workings of anyone's mind, so who am I to judge? It's a mystery to me—and I don't have any good answers.

While I was there, my mother and I attended a meeting for the Feng Shui Institute of the Midwest. My mom only knew about feng shui because I had been raving about my experiences with it while I was in Seattle. After learning about this practice, I had become very involved with studying the ideas and was eager to learn more. She was astonished when she noticed a flyer for this club's annual meeting on the bulletin board at her local fitness center. The program we attended was fascinating. When I returned home from Minnesota, I decided to see if there was a similar society in Connecticut. There was one, The New England School of Feng Shui. I went to the website and was astounded to see that Denise Linn would be teaching an upcoming weekend course. According to my teachers in Seattle, Denise was the guru of feng shui. It turned out that she had only taught at this school once before, several years earlier, and she most likely would never teach there again.

I attended the weekend. However, Denise was not teaching feng shui, but rather her philosophy on Soul Coaching®. I decided to remain open and let Universe lead me where It wanted me to go. Suffice it to say, this was a wise decision. I was blown away by her personal stories and how she guided us in learning how to tap into our soul, as our soul knows the truth. Denise took us on guided meditations to meet our higher selves, spirit guides, even ourselves in past lives, and we discovered how to find answers for ourselves. It was life-changing. I reached out into the Universe, remained open, and I was rewarded.

After attending a few more classes at the New England school, I decided to use feng shui to help shift my energy to find a job. I realized that the area outside my home that represented my career was a patch of land filled with weeds and void of any character or direction—a respectable representation of my current situation. I hired a landscape designer to create a plan, using the principles of feng shui. Within a week of me writing the check for the completion of the work, which included a waterfall feature and gorgeous plantings, I received a call from a headhunter.

"Hi, Lisa. I'm not quite sure how I received your résumé, but I wanted to connect with you as I am looking to fill a position. Your qualifications look perfect. I can't give you the name of the company, but it's local, at a hedge fund. It's in the accounting department, and they're looking for someone part-time. The pay is very generous. I was wondering if you'd be interested in applying?"

I was dumbfounded. Almost a year earlier I had sent out a few résumés, but had no response. And here it was, a week after completing a feng shui "cure" in my career section and seemingly out of nowhere I receive a call for the exact job I had wanted earlier? Even the headhunter sounded surprised. I interviewed a few days later.

Here's the rub. After attending Denise's program I had signed up for her Soul Coaching® school in Paso Robles, California. I was to leave in a few days for a ten day course. When I signed up for the class, I had no idea I might be offered a position back in accounting.

Three days later, when I landed in Los Angeles, to change planes, I received a phone call from the controller of the company offering me the position.

Even though it appeared to be the answer to my prayers, I was torn about accepting it. My soul was calling me to pursue a more spiritual path, but my ego was not ready to bare my soul to the world. I had been out of the work world for a while, so my confidence level was decidedly low. I wasn't sure I remembered my debits and credits, let alone how to help someone on their spiritual path. I was still fumbling along on my own journey—*was I really ready to help others on theirs?* I wasn't so sure. I reluctantly accepted the accounting position.

I returned from studying with Denise as a Certified Soul Coach and Past Life Coach. The next day I started at the hedge fund. The same day, September 16, 2008, the markets began their downward spiral—the day after Wall Street giant Lehman Brothers had gone bankrupt, which would be the "Big Bang" of the coming recession. Things continued to plummet fast, leading up to the October 2008 crash. It was clear that the signs were pointing in one direction regarding my future—it could not have been a more inauspicious day to start working in finance. Several people were let go from the firm. Luckily, I was not one of them. I continued working there for a year and a half, with the intention of eventually quitting to pursue my soul-coaching dream.

While I was at Denise's training, I made very good friends with all the people in my class. There were sixteen of us. Denise called us the Bamboos because we were each individual stocks of strength and growth, yet we liked to be connected to grow and learn together, like a grove of bamboo. I had shared with the group my connection with the angels and how I could channel them. They were all fascinated by this.

After the class, a few Bamboo friends occasionally asked me to channel an answer from the angels for a particular question. I always did this via email. I was used to writing down the angels' messages when I channeled for myself. I was not channeling for money yet, just helping my friends out with questions that they had. It felt like a natural thing to do.

One of the women, Barb, lived in London. She came to my home for a visit. We were chatting, and she asked me if she could ask the angels a question. I told her I'd have to get a pad and pencil.

"Can't I just ask the question, and then you just directly tell me the answer, without writing it down? You know, just speak what they say?"

"I've never thought of doing that before. Okay, let's give it a try."

We sat on the guest-room floor, facing each other. I closed my eyes. "Okay, what's your question?"

"I want to know about the direction of my life. Am I on the right path?"

Suddenly, I felt as though a train dropped on my head. This huge rush of energy poured right into that spot.

When I spoke, it didn't feel like me at all. "Welcome, Barb. We are glad you are here and are very happy to answer your question." My voice sounded like a robot, mechanical and halting. "We want you to know that you are on your path and that…" The energy wouldn't stop. My teeth started to chatter, and I felt as though I was floating or being lifted off of the ground. My entire body was vibrating and my neck became stiff. No words were coming out; a rush of energy, like a lightning bolt, was coming through the top of my head.

I called out to Barb, "Make them stop! Make them go away!" I tried to push the words out of my mouth, because I felt as though I had no control over my body. "Tell them to go away!"

Barb said, "Stop! Angels, stop! She wants you to leave." As quickly as the energy rushed in, it rushed out. I felt light-headed and disoriented.

"Oh my God, Lisa. Are you okay?" Barb asked.

I rubbed my forehead. "Oh God, I'm okay. I just need some water. That was crazy. I've never felt that way before. It was a rush, but scary too."

Having the angels' energy enter my body was mind-blowing. When I wrote down their messages on paper, the energy felt lightly connected; yet, when I opened myself up to channel the message through my voice, it was as though

I became an untethered live electrical wire. The experience reminded me of the time I touched the glowing red wire in a toaster with a knife.

I was six years old and making myself some cinnamon sugar toast. As I stared down into the toaster, I saw the dark wires begin to turn red and I became curious as to what would happen if I touched one of them with a butter knife. I picked up the knife and gently touched it to the red coil. The electricity instantly shot through my arm and down through my body. I screamed the loudest scream of my life. My dad, who was outside on a ladder, rushed to my side and sprained his ankle in the process. The fright of it scared me more than the electrical shock, but the repairman told my mom that if I'd been holding something wet, like a damp sponge, I could have been killed.

Connecting so directly with the angels opened a door inside of me that I didn't know existed. Feeling that kind of energy enter my body was exciting and indescribably loving; yet the thoughts that tumbled through my head were shattering. Was this for real? Was I making this up? What on earth was happening? I was my own biggest skeptic. I felt as though I was about to have a panic attack. My friend Barb was able to calm me down and help me come back to feeling like my normal self.

After that experience, I learned how to ground myself and how to ask the angels to come, and then go, gently. They were likely just excited that I had finally, after five years, decided to try another way of communicating with them. Over the next year, I would occasionally channel, both in writing and in person, with my friends and family. Everyone I gave a message to seemed to enjoy the guidance and loving advice. But I was being pulled in two directions; the spiritual and the practical. As my hedge fund job became more demanding, I found less and less time to connect to Spirit. It was all due to come to a head.

At some point the next year, I was asked to increase my work hours from part-time to full-time, twenty-five to fifty hours a week. I was working in the accounting department, and eventually I took on the role of ensuring the company's tax compliance. This was about as far from spiritual work as I could get. Working in a toxic environment of greed and hostility was taking its toll. I noticed that Spirit was making it more and more difficult for me to work there. I didn't want to leave—the money was too good—yet the tensions in the office grew thicker and thicker every day.

In particular, there was one woman who irritated me. It wasn't just me, either; she enjoyed tormenting everyone. I couldn't understand why my supervisors allowed this woman to so blatantly abuse people with her remarks and actions. It built up inside of me, until one day I had had enough. She found an entry in QuickBooks that I had entered incorrectly. Rather than just fixing the problem by clicking on the delete button, she called me on the phone from her desk. She sat *three desks* from mine.

"Lisa. I just noticed you entered an erroneous QuickBooks entry in one of the accounts. I have gotten out of the program so you can go in and delete it."

It was simply the last straw. After being worn down again and again by her constant finger pointing and manipulation, I was done.

I hung up, took a deep breath and went to her desk.

"Janie! You are insane! What is *your* problem?" I bellowed. "You couldn't just delete it, and tell me later? No, you couldn't do that! You *know* that I'm working on a deadline to get the tax shit out the door? And on top of it, I saw that you just emailed my bosses about it? What have I ever done to you?" I was livid.

She looked at me calmly and said, "Well, you are obviously going to be a terrible soul coach with an attitude like that. You won't be able to help anyone."

I turned on my heels and walked straight into the human resource director's office, just beyond my desk. My friend Abbey was hiding in the office with Morgan, the HR director. I deliberately placed both of my hands on her door and slammed it shut with every ounce of force in my body. The building shook. Abbey and Morgan were frozen in their seats. They were trying not to laugh, because they had never seen me like this. My face was red, and I felt as if steam was coming out of my ears. I looked at Abbey and hot, searing tears poured out of my eyes. There was a vent in Morgan's ceiling that connected to a vent just above Janie's desk. I knew that Janie used this opening to eavesdrop on Morgan's office.

"How dare you tell me I won't be a good soul coach! I fucking HATE you!" I screamed toward the vent.

Now, I was not proud of that moment. It was not me at my best, obviously. However, in retrospect I'm grateful for that experience. I'm grateful for Janie, as she helped me to clearly see that I should no longer be working in that environment. I put in my notice that day. Two weeks later I was done. I was so excited, yet terrified to finally be done at the hedge fund.

As a side note, about three years later, the newspapers reported that a federal grand jury handed down a nineteen-count indictment charging three executives of this hedge fund with conspiracy, securities fraud, and wire fraud offenses. If convicted, the executives are looking at a combined sentence of two hundred years in prison. I guess Spirit was looking out for me more than I knew....

I was free at last and immediately started my *Art of Living Happy* blog. Once again, Universe had put me where I needed to be.

CHAPTER 7

But a clean break was not so easy. It never is. The hedge fund offered me a $10,000 bonus if I stayed an extra two months. They bought my soul for two additional months; I figured the money would help seed my new business.

The evening of my last day at work, I invited every "spiritual" person I knew to my house for my very first goddess energy circle. My plan was to host a monthly energy circle, focusing on a different goddess each time. It was the eve of May Day, and the great goddess Flora, the Roman goddess of spring and flowers, was the perfect goddess to discuss. I made twelve 4 x 6 laminated cards with a picture of Flora on one side and a description of who she was on the back. I planned a fire ceremony, a mock maypole and a light dinner.

After playing a role at the hedge fund that felt unnatural to me, I finally could be myself. My excitement was palpable. On that last day, I arrived home from work, quickly changed out of my accounting garb, khakis and a button-down shirt—it felt like shedding skin. I changed into a white silk tunic lightly adorned with silver sequins. I could feel myself leaving one life behind for another, trading one persona for a new one that fit me better. I finished the preparations and anxiously waited for the dozen or so people I had invited to arrive.

Unfortunately, only two people showed up: Laurie and Tiffany. I was crushed.

I had recently met Laurie at an Isis initiation event. I had no idea what an Isis initiation event was, except that a tarot reader I had met had recommended the two-day workshop when I sought advice on how to go deeper into my spiritual path. At the event, Laurie and I quickly realized we lived just down the street from one another, which was interesting given that the event was forty-five minutes away. On the second day, as we drove to the event together, she told me she had joined the Hare Krishnas as a young woman and that she ultimately entered into an arranged marriage and had three children. Realizing that she didn't want the same life for her kids, she left the Krishnas. Her revelations were profound. Never had I known anyone with a life so different from mine. She went on to get her degree at Columbia University and put her three kids through college. Her story was inspirational.

I met Tiffany walking her toy poodle one day while I was doing some errands in town. She recently moved to the area and was renting a small cottage at the back of one of the big homes on Main Street. It turned out that she was an energy healer at one of the well-known metaphysical book stores in a neighboring town. I wasn't really surprised as she had that vibe; she was a large-ish woman with wild black hair and blond highlights. Her wardrobe (from all I'd seen) primarily consisted of long flowing dresses.

Tiffany and Laurie had made appetizers, and I showed them to the kitchen. I noted my reaction to Tiffany. Her fashion sense and her size were typical of certain women in the spiritual community. In truth, Tiffany brought up major fears in me regarding the image people have of the "spiritual type." In movies and on TV, psychics, tarot card readers, channelers and other kinds of spiritual people are typically portrayed as witch-like, heavyset women with unruly hair and a house full of cats. I felt mean thinking this, but most of the spiritual healers or teachers I knew *were* pretty out there. I loved learning what they had to teach, but as a successful corporate accountant, I guess I thought I was above them, or at least I certainly didn't want to be lumped into their category.

I felt how judgmental this was and how I was slapping not only Tiffany, but an entire community, across the face for being authentic—*which was exactly what I was trying to be*. It was horrible, but I was still having a hard time envisioning being spiritual; if I had to be like Tiffany, I guess I didn't want to be. As a spiritual person, I knew that we were all one, and it was wrong to judge, but my ego couldn't help how it felt.

After several minutes of small talk, waiting to see if anyone else would show up, I nervously asked them to come outside onto my deck so we could begin the evening. I had bought some sage and was going to start off by lighting the sage and smudging each person before they entered the house. Before spiritual practices, it's customary to cleanse negativity and purify the space around your body and your aura.

I set the pottery bowl and the feather down on my outside table and began trying to light the sage with a match. I felt Tiffany and Laurie's eyes on me as I struggled. Running through my head was the fact that only two of my friends showed up; none of the others seemed to care about this huge step in my life. To top it off, I couldn't even light the goddamn sage. Tiffany walked over and took the lighter and sage out of my hand. "Here, let me do that. It looks like you're having a problem."

I willingly turned the sage over to the wiser one and let her take it from there. My self-confidence had been shattered, so I just let her. She removed the cord wrapped around the sage and broke strands of the herb into the pottery bowl. Then when she touched a match to it, the sage immediately caught fire. Soon it was smoldering. A generous amount of sage smoke wafted into the air.

"Lisa, come stand in front of me," she said. She took the feather and began directing the sage in front of me and around my back. She saged to the east, south, west, and north. She raised the sage up to the Sun and then down to Mother Earth. She asked God, the Angels and the Universe to help cleanse away any negativity that surrounded me and to replace it with positive energy. She then went on to sage Laurie and then Laurie smudged Tiffany.

"Okay. Let's go in and eat," Tiffany said as she opened the door, walking straight for the two appetizers sitting on the counter. "Oh, and Lisa," she picked up one of the bruschetta pieces from the plate and started bringing it up to her mouth, "After dinner, I was thinking that for practice why don't you channel for Laurie and me?"

"Um, okay," I replied. There went my entire evening plans. In a flash, they were scrapped.

I channeled for her and Laurie for almost an hour.

After Tiffany left, Laurie stayed. "Lisa, I'm curious. Why did you let Tiffany *take over* like that?"

"I guess because I really don't know what I'm doing," I said, loading the plates into the dishwasher.

Laurie was wiping the counter. "I think you need to step up to your own power. You're amazing. You've just got to believe it." It was valuable advice that I took to heart.

That was the first and last goddess energy circle.

Later that night I was thinking about what had gone wrong. Wondering why I somehow thought that by quitting my accounting job, which I had come to hate, and starting a goddess circle, I would somehow be magically transported into the land of spirituality. Like I could just shift overnight—literally—and become someone and something new.

The reality was a smack in the face; I still had a lot of internal work to do. I needed to first believe in myself before I moved on to anything else. I needed to stop letting people tell me what to do and how to do it. I needed to own this amazing gift that had been bestowed upon me. A necessary part of the process was that I had to redefine my past trauma in a spiritual light; this would help me gain a new perspective. Finally, I needed to figure out what it was I was really here to do.

By the end of the night, I'd made a decision. I would move forward and focus on starting out on my own.

During the next several weeks I immersed myself in how to go about doing that, first focusing on starting my own business. The truth was that I didn't have a business model. All I knew was that I was being pushed, or rather pulled, into creating this business by a force that was greater than me. I knew I couldn't continue working in the corporate world, as the energy and toxicity of the environment was killing me from the inside out, just as it had done to Ian.

Days before Ian died he made a confession to me. At the time it broke my heart, but as the years went by his words began to haunt me. It wasn't until I approached my forty-fourth birthday (seven years after his death and the same age at which he died) that his words would have the most impact on me. He told me that he regretted his career choice. He wished he had chosen to be a doctor so he could have helped more people. He felt his time as a tax attorney had been wasted as he mainly helped corporations save money. What did that do for humanity? He said he felt the societal pressure to climb the corporate ladder for his own financial success was a fraud to his personal happiness. Knowing that I would be living even one day longer than him made me realize I didn't want to come to the end of my life wishing I had done something else so that I could have helped more people—this was my chance to do just that.

My life had already grown so much fuller because of my connection to Spirit; it allowed me to meet David; it provided me with the home of my dreams; it turned even the most mundane daily experiences into magic. With Spirit anything and everything felt possible—it was like nothing I had ever experienced. My world had gone from low-resolution black and white to full-on high definition color. I felt compelled to share this knowledge with the world. It became an obsession.

I knew that I wanted to channel healing messages for people, as I had received such great feedback from my friends and the few people who had allowed me to share my "gift" at the Isis initiation. I thought of the word *gift* in quotes, because I felt that the channeling I did was something anyone who was interested could do—especially if they were dedicated and willing to practice as long as I had, which by this point was eight years.

It was like playing the piano; some people were natural piano players and the ones who weren't could practice and get better. I also wanted to incorporate the professional training as a soul coach I had received from Denise Linn, as well as my feng shui and space clearing knowledge. Essentially, I wanted to share with others what I had learned: How connecting to Spirit could change their life for the better and that there were unlimited ways in which Spirit was willing to meet them on their path. There was no *one* right way.

I signed up for a continuing education course called "How to Write a Business Plan." It was a bit of a waste of time, to be honest. Being an accountant, I already knew pretty much everything they taught. I was looking for more sage advice as to how to actually start a business channeling angels and giving spiritual advice. The one thing I did learn was how to register my business name, Art of Living Happy, LLC, with the State of Connecticut. Making it official and legal was a great first step.

About six weeks after I quit my job, I attended an all day workshop on "How to Become a Channeler." It was taught by Roland Comtois, a well-known medium in the New England area. Laurie told me about the class and went with me. She had gone to one of his live events a couple of weeks earlier and had received a very loving message from her mother who had passed away earlier in the year. I knew I wanted one of his readings.

When we arrived at Star Visions, a spiritual healing center about thirty minutes away in New York, there were about twenty women there. Roland started the class and spoke for about five minutes. Then, in the midst of his speech, he stopped mid-sentence. He turned on his heel and walked across the front of the room and stood in front of where I was sitting. He pointed at me in the second row.

"Why are you here?" he asked.

I froze. I felt like I was on the spot, or I'd been caught doing something.

"You are already a channeler," he said.

"Uh, I…I want to learn more about how to make a business of it," I hesitantly replied.

"I see Archangel Michael standing right behind you, as if he's guarding you. You don't even realize how powerful you are. You just need to step into the work. It's waiting there for you." He went back to his lecture.

I sat there in astonishment. I thought about how I call on Archangel Michael every single time I do my work. I ask him to stand behind me and guard me to keep me safe. If only I could believe in myself as much as everyone else did, including Archangel Michael.

I then worked with an Internet marketing professional. Clay was super-enthusiastic and supportive of my new blog about spiritual ideas. However, he'd never worked with anyone spiritual before. His great ideas, like flashing links on my page, probably worked wonders for the people selling Viagra or quickie diet fixes, but I was skeptical about it for what I was trying to do. Clay was so helpful and generous with his time and attention that I didn't want to hurt his feelings by telling him no.

For three months, I was on a high. I had started my own business, and I was writing my blog every day. I had a sophisticated website that was going to bring in a ton of money—I was just sure of it.

Then…nothing. Somehow I thought that the minute I launched, everyone in the world would start reading it. My friends and family wondered why a spiritual website would have blinking, flashing ads. Some of the information that I posted about myself was so revealing, so raw and personal that I didn't sleep for days after posting. My spiritual side was aching to reach out and connect. I was looking for anyone who could relate to what I had gone through, to understand what kind of hell I had been in. How connecting to the angels and my inner light had set me free.

Not only was I free, but also I was flourishing in life and in love. After connecting to Spirit, my life had expanded into a multidimensional space. I had never felt so alive. The best part is that it was so easy—if only I could tell more people. That's all I wanted, to help anyone suffering from the death of a loved one, or even suffering from the spiritual deadening of a mundane life.

In reality, though, I was a mess. I could barely say the word *spirituality* without breaking into a cold sweat. I knew that my path had helped me, and I did want to share it, yet I was terrified. I was afraid of what people would think. For god's sake, I was a certified public accountant. *What was I doing talking to angels?!*

In mid-August, we flew to Ireland for a week's vacation to visit David's family. It was just what I needed. I was feeling stressed about the fact that nothing was really happening with my new path, so it was refreshing to get out of the country. It was the first time we had gone to Ireland in the summer. We stayed with David's sister at Brittis

Bay, a beachfront community where David had spent his boyhood summers. It was a magical trip; we were rewarded with blue skies and sun and the views were spectacular. David took us to his secret fishing spots and walked us along the shore, telling us stories of his childhood.

When we returned, I dropped into such a deep depression that I could barely get out of bed. I usually unpacked within a day or two of returning from a trip, but this time I just let the clothes stay in the suitcase. In fact, I began throwing additional clothes on top of the suitcase. My closet became a dumping ground. I would fish through the mountain to find a reasonably clean outfit. I stopped showering daily. I felt there was no reason for me to be here. I never actually contemplated suicide, but I truly just didn't want to be here on this earth anymore. What had I done? I had thrown away a lucrative job to do what? Tell people how I talked to angels? How they helped me find my husband and a beautiful new home? Who would care? *Why was I here? What the hell was I doing?*

One of the most difficult aspects of my new path was that I no longer had anyone telling me what to do. Every day I had to figure out what I needed to do to keep my business moving forward. It was the same way when I left the church. In so many ways, it was easier to be dictated to by others. And yet, that was the problem.

I had allowed myself to become dependent on what others told me. I no longer knew what was inside of me, what I really wanted to do with my life. As a child, it was following what my parents told me to do, then it was the teachers, and then it was society in general. I had become addicted to allowing others to do the thinking, feeling and being for me. In essence, I had turned into a zombie.

When I was working at the hedge fund, I would get up, go to work, come home, eat dinner, watch TV, and go to bed. The next day would be the same. My mind would be numb from the lack of creativity, and I would continue to spiral further away from my true being. It wasn't until I was out on my own for a few months that I realized that I had to figure out all of this *for myself.* Then I panicked.

After a few weeks of wallowing in this feeling of uselessness, I decided to give up my spiritual business and look for a part-time job. I perused the town's weekly newspaper and found a posting for a part-time clerical position at the local Board of Realtors. I sent my résumé in and was called for an interview. Ten minutes into the interview, my cell phone rang. It was Jenna, my daughter. She had been involved in a car accident. She assured me she was fine and that it wasn't her fault. She was very shaken and didn't know what to do next—she had just gotten her license. I found out she was only a few minutes from where I was and told her to wait for me. I explained to the director that I wouldn't be able to finish the interview and that I had to leave immediately.

When I arrived at the scene I was astonished at what I saw. Jenna was perfectly fine. Her car had a slight scratch on the rear bumper, but the front end of the other driver's car was demolished. He'd driven through a stop sign.

The angels later explained to me that they had to get my attention. They knew I would have taken the easy way out by accepting the clerical position (which I was offered, even though I didn't finish the interview), deterring me even longer from my life's work here on earth.

They got my attention.

CHAPTER 8

I was scared out of my mind. I wasn't ready for this. I was about walk into a place of business and ask them to let me do angel readings for customers, total strangers. I was about to take a giant step forward on my path.

Awakenings in Katonah, New York, is a sweet store filled with crystals, books, jewelry and a palpable, pleasing energy. You're immediately greeted with mystical burning incense. Then your eyes are drawn to the powerful art on the walls and the crystals carefully placed around the store. The space is also filled with books that cover an expansive array of spiritual teachings and lessons. I was relieved that the owner, Linda Love, was extremely receptive to my offer. She explained that she was going to be out of town the following week and was too busy to schedule a test reading. She'd never hired someone before without experiencing their work, but she said she could feel that my energy was authentic, and sensed that I would work well there. Linda was about to give me my first opportunity to get paid to follow my path. And she had no idea whether or not I knew what I was doing. She took a leap of faith in me—now I just had to do it.

The following Friday I went to the store, set up my table in the back room with my cards, some essential rose oil and a spray bottle filled with a mixture of essential oils. Just before going to Ireland, I had received a message from the angels to go online and look up essential oils, as I was to use them in my work. I came across Alaska Essences, a company that creates healing essences from various aspects of nature. They have a line of sacred space-clearing sprays, one of which is called "Calling All Angels." This spray helps you connect to the love, guidance and protection of the angelic realm. Included in the formula are angelica, chalice well, chiming bells and kunzite. I felt a warm tingle in my body when I read on their website that these formulas were created after studying feng shui and space clearing with Denise Linn. Since Denise was my teacher when I became a certified soul coach, everything was aligning perfectly.

I then sat and waited. Those opposing forces were again pulling me, as I was simultaneously petrified and exhilarated. When my first client arrived, a voice went off in my head: *What am I doing? Do I really think that I can do this?* I just kept going, turning on my music and asking the client to take a deep breath and relax. The advice was more for me than for her! My heart was pounding and my palms were sweating.

I then started as I always do when I'm working by myself, shuffling my oracle cards. I asked the client to pick three cards. The first card indicated blocks, the second advice for clearing the blockage and the third was the outcome card. The client and I then talked a bit about how these cards were relevant to her life. I also explained that the more open she was, the better connection I would get with her soul, as well as with the angels and spirits that wished to come through.

A lot has changed for me since that first reading, but one thing that has remained is I continue to be worried that I'm going to get something wrong. There is also a feeling that I have to prove to people that what's happening is real. I'm my own biggest critic; ironically, the most skeptical person I have to deal with in all of this is myself.

My brain had been trained to think in a linear fashion and to have proof for everything—a remnant from my old life as an accountant. I think I liked accounting so much because it was safe and predictable. There was always a right answer; after all, it was just math. There was a comfort in it—the unknown was thrilling, but it also came with an uncertainty that could be terrifying.

When I did my spirit work for myself, I could accept what information I received because I could literally feel that what I was getting was the truth. When I started working with other people, I became frightened of being judged, being ridiculed or just being plain wrong. This was my deepest fear, which at times paralyzed me from working with other people.

I've been a people pleaser all of my life and, of course, I now wanted to please my clients. I've had to learn to step out of the way and let Spirit do the work—not to judge what the client got or didn't get. No matter how much discomfort I have when working with others, I know that the gift I have is to be shared.

I recited an invocation to invite beings of love and light who wanted to assist with the reading: Angels, archangels, spirit guides, ascended masters, my ancestors and guides, as well as the client's higher self, guides, and ancestors. I asked to be a clear channel to bring through the most helpful, loving guidance that the person needed to hear to move forward in life. I felt a shift deep within me, as though my thinking brain stepped to the side.

What happened next was a true gift from Spirit. Spirit came to tell the client how much she was loved. We here on Earth have no idea how much love there truly is for us—not only out in the Universe, but more important, *within us.* The problem is that so many of us have buried the access to our own love because of all the difficulties we've experienced. I gave the client an overview of what was going on in her life.

Then the angels opened up the floor to the client to ask whatever questions she wanted answered. I'm always astounded at the information that comes through.

Though the specifics of this first reading escape me, I do remember that after she was done, she thanked me profusely for all the information. I felt lifted and vindicated. There is no better feeling than actually tapping into the divine and your sacred work here on earth.

****

Touch of Sedona was the name of the store where I'd received my very first angel message years earlier; it was also where I'd gotten the name of the space clearer who helped me sell my house. I approached the owner, Marge, about doing readings out of her store. Interestingly, her regular Friday reader had recently given notice due to a family emergency, so Marge invited me to begin working right away.

As wonderful as it was to be doing the spiritual readings at Touch of Sedona, the real reason I believe I was led there was to connect with Marge. Every Friday was different. Some days I would have back-to-back readings and other days no one came in. In these quiet moments, Marge and I would talk. She was like my soul mother. She had fine, feathery, short white hair and an infectious, playful attitude. She was deeply intuitive and loved what she did. She actually reminded me of a sprite—a wispy, delicate fairy.

I was amazed at how much we had in common. She was widowed (actually twice), losing her first husband to cancer, her second to a heart attack. My house was across the street from where she lived with her second husband, before he passed.

Although she was considerably older than I, we communicated like sisters. We shared many of our deepest fears, dreams and experiences. I'll always have a special feeling of love for Marge more than she could ever imagine. She was there at the beginning, and embraced me when I was vulnerable.

The greatest gift Marge gave me was a simple one, but one I desperately needed: She took me seriously. She gave me permission to be myself and explore this gift, which I was so unsure of how to share. She encouraged me with remarks like, "Oh, Lisa. I could really see a positive shift in energy with your last client. I don't know what you said, but I could just see a difference in their demeanor." She would also validate my intuitive hits by confirming information that I would receive from seemingly out of nowhere. As my spiritual mediumship blossomed, Marge was my greatest cheerleader and guide.

I started getting into the routine of doing the readings every Friday. Most times the reading went really well, and the client was thrilled or relieved with what I had told them. Yet, there were times when I would get nothing. I have a vivid memory of a client reluctantly walking into the tiny room, sitting down at the table in front of me and saying in a stern voice, "Okay, read me." I was taken aback, as no one had ever approached me so confrontationally.

I set the timer for fifteen minutes and stated my opening invocation. I waited. A minute or two went by, and I literally got nothing. Inside my head, I pleaded with the angels to help me. My heart began to pound and my hands were sweating. On the inside, I was panicked, completely freaking out. I took a deep breath.

The spirits must have guided me as, out of nowhere, I politely asked the client to please uncross her arms. I then explained that part of connecting to the spirit world is being able to connect *through* the person I'm reading for. Once I explained that, the woman let down her guard, and I was able to give her a short reading that she was quite pleased with. I made it, but it was during these times I would get really down on myself and berate myself for not being good enough. I hadn't yet learned the lesson that it wasn't about me; I was just the messenger, and the client always got the perfect message—and sometimes that meant no message.

For the most part, the messages were filled with love and light. Most people wanted to know about their career, their love life, or their finances. One day, a new client walked in, and I started the reading. I suddenly got a very intense message that this woman's daughter was involved with an evil man. I was reluctant to share this—I had never had a message like this before, so I hesitated.

"I'm not quite sure how to say this…"

"Please, tell me anything," the client pleaded.

"Well, I'm getting that your daughter is involved with someone that is…is evil." I cringed as I said this.

She hit the table with her hand. "I knew it!"

"I have to tell you, I've never read someone and gotten this type of overwhelmingly negative information before. It's…uncomfortable. I mean it's uncomfortable for me to share with you." I was entering unfamiliar territory.

"This is why I came. I'm so worried about my daughter, and I was hoping the angels could help me help her. Please…please go on."

I focused and reconnected to Spirit. "You must put together a prayer circle of friends and family to pray for your daughter. Visualize a golden light and envision your daughter walking toward it. She is lost and must find her way back to the light. You will be able to help her. The angels and the realms of love and light appreciate the care and concern you have for her. Know that you are blessed and filled with the love and light of God."

As she left the room, I felt a cold dreary invisible cloud descend upon my head. I tried to shake it off and told myself that I was just imagining things. However, that night I took the feeling home with me, and I couldn't sleep; I was tossing and turning. After several hours, I thought I was having a panic attack or even a heart attack. I got out of bed and walked downstairs to the kitchen. I thought I'd feel better if I grounded myself by eating something. I finally asked my angels to release me from whatever it was that was holding me hostage.

Almost immediately I felt the grip loosen. I later realized that I had picked up some negative energy from my client earlier that day. I had become a psychic sponge. The dark side knew I was spreading love and light, so I was an easy and open target. As I channeled more and more, I learned ways to protect my clients, my house, my loved ones and myself from these negative energies.

When I first ventured into spiritual work, I was totally unaware of the importance of grounding and self-protection. During various intuitive readings that I attended, the practitioner would tell me that I needed to develop a self-protection practice as I deepened my study of Spirit. I didn't realize the importance of this until I had negative entities invade my space. This can be scary, if you allow it to be, however, it comes with the territory. One just has to prepare for it and learn various ways to defend against it.

Over time I developed the ritual of asking Archangel Michael to stand behind me, Archangel Raphael to stand to my right, Archangel Gabriel to stand to my left and Archangel Ariel to stand in front of me. I had my spirit animal, a dragon, stand above me and my Fire Goddess stand below me, tending the fire that burns with my desire to work with Spirit. I asked for fireflies to illuminate the inside of me and asked for dragonflies to guide me to the entities of love and light.

In order to ground myself onto the earth, I would ask for a ray of sunshine to shine forth from the heavens, to travel down through my head and my other chakras, to pass down through my tailbone into the floor below me, all the way down into the deep crystals of the earth. I would ask this, either to myself or aloud, every time that I embarked on working with Spirit. Sometimes it worked, and sometimes it didn't.

And as much as I only wanted to work with love and light, occasionally I would pick up a negative vibe; then I would have to work on ridding myself of this entity. Self-protection has been a long journey for me. Trying to understand the boundaries around channeling and working with Spirit has been challenging. I continue to discover ways to help me better protect and ground myself for a deeper and more meaningful connection to Spirit.

It was interesting how my opening to Spirit affected my children. Jenna was especially intrigued with the work.

One day she asked if she could get some tarot cards. Although the tarot never resonated with me, I had a couple of decks and a book in my meditation room, and invited her in to look at them.

Jenna was able to pick up on the nuances of the tarot cards immediately. It was as though I had built a swimming pool by opening myself up to spiritual work, and she decided to jump in and start swimming on her own. I spoke freely about my communication with angels from the beginning, not cramming it down my kids' throats, but also I wasn't shy about exposing them to the spiritual work and channeling I was doing.

Around this time, I invited Jenna to a Shaman workshop on finding your spirit animal. It was a magical experience. There were maybe six participants. Our leader explained that we would be journeying to meet our spirit animal. She began beating a drum, as though it were a heartbeat, and then told us to go meet our guide. I envisioned a deep forest; my animal was a fierce dragon, ready to protect me at any time. Jenna's animal was an elk. The teacher had found an elk vertebrae many years earlier and gave it to Jenna, who has it to this day.

Robbie, who was fourteen by this point, was understandably less interested. I think boys in general are less attracted to the spirit world—maybe because of societal pressures and gender expectations. However, ever since his father died, he had been experiencing Spirit on a daily basis and probably didn't want any more overt experiences than he already had. After Ian's death, Robbie's room continually had issues with lights flickering, his fan running by itself and the radio mysteriously clicking on. What I find so interesting about this is that when Ian was a child he reported the *exact same type of occurrences* to his mother. Ian saw and heard spirits throughout his childhood, but he never wanted to discuss it more than he absolutely had to.

****

In early 2011, I took a Hay House cruise to the Caribbean. Hay House publishes self-help and spiritual books. On the cruise, some of their top authors hosted seminars: Dr. Wayne Dyer, Gregg Braden, Sonia Choquette, John Holland, Caroline Myss, Cheryl Richardson, Dr. Brian Weiss and my mentor, Denise Linn. The experience was amazing, as everyone on board was like minded. Denise conducted a past-life seminar. She led a past-life regression where I saw myself as the fat woman in a traveling carnival. I wore a yellow polka-dotted dress with a peplum. My body was so obese I could barely sit on the stool inside my caged wagon. People threw tomatoes and other rotten produce at me. I sat there and stared blankly at them as they yelled profanities. The humiliation was palpable.

After returning from the cruise, I realized something profound: Deep inside, I was feeling just like that caged fat woman in my current life. I was scared that people viewed me as a freak, or a spectacle—something to make fun of and ridicule. To change this feeling I decided to also see clients on a more intimate basis out of a space in my home. I turned a sunroom into a dedicated meditation room, filling it with crystals, spiritual paintings, candles, sheer ivory curtains and a delicate pink chandelier—a perfect place to see clients privately.

Working from a beautiful room surrounded by windows with views of the lake, trees and flowers made a huge difference. I was able to delve much deeper into the connection to Spirit without feeling so vulnerable.

One of my very first clients at the house, Barbara, gave me a gift that allowed me to open up even more. I started her reading like all the others. We talked about what was going on in her life, and then I had her pull three cards. I read the three cards, which were right on the money. Then the angels asked me to see if she'd be willing to allow me to place my hands on her shoulders. She agreed. After placing my hands on her, I opened my channel.

"Oh my God! Angels! The room is filled with angels!" she gasped.

Based on our brief conversation, I knew that Barbara was a real believer in angels and connected to them on a regular basis, but she was not a channeler. We both were genuinely shocked that she saw angels.

"What? Really?" I stammered as I looked around the room and saw nothing.

"I just can't get over it. I see angels everywhere. They're so beautiful!"

I wasn't sure if my client was having a stroke, or if she was really seeing angels. I truly am my biggest skeptic.

"Wait—who is that standing there? In a Yankees T-shirt? He's got blue jeans and white socks. No shoes."

At first I was confused. Then I got excited. "What color is his hair? What does he look like?" I asked.

"He's got dark blond hair, a square face. Longish. He's thin. He's got...a blue hoodie over his shoulder."

"Oh, my god! That's Michael!" Michael was a golf assistant of David's who was killed in a house fire two years earlier. "He worked with my husband!"

"Mike is nodding...he's nodding his head yes. He's giving the thumbs up sign. His energy is so playful! Wait, he just got really serious. He's talking: 'Lisa, believe in yourself. You have this gift. Quit doubting yourself. Your gift will grow. You are going to continue to open and start connecting to people who have passed away. Your gift is going to help heal so many people, just believe!'"

At that moment I didn't know if I should be paying my client for sharing this message with me or rejoicing in having heard it. Hearing this message from Michael was a turning point in my spiritual and career development.

Soon after, the president of the chamber of commerce stopped by Touch of Sedona, and I gave her a reading. I ended up joining and getting a booth at the showcase of the local chamber of commerce members. I purchased some adorable plush angel dolls to sell at my table as well as some silk scarves, which I blessed with angelic energy. Once again, by putting more of myself out there, things began to happen.

The director of the Ridgefield Playhouse stopped by to talk to me about the type of work I did and then asked if I'd be interested in sponsoring Gabrielle Bernstein, an up-and-coming spiritual teacher from New York City who was scheduled to speak at the Playhouse. I'd be featured on the advertising and be given a table where I could sell items and do readings on the night of the event. I was nervous and scared, as it was going to cost money and it would involve really putting myself out there. After giving it some thought, I said yes.

The night of the event, I showed up with my deck of cards, my essential oils, dolls and scarves and began giving free readings to anyone who wanted one. I was fortunate enough to be given a table right next to where Gabrielle was selling her newly released book. The next thing I knew, two dozen people were standing in a line waiting for a reading. People were blown away by what I was telling them. It was so easy and so fun! The Playhouse director asked for a reading and was so impressed, she asked if I wanted to do my own show the following March. *Did I want to do my own show? This was something I'd only imagined in my dreams—another miracle!*

Once I learned I was going to have my own show, I realized that I needed some more practice. I asked my friend LJ if she would help me set up some home events. LJ and I had met at the Isis Initiation almost a year earlier, and she was very supportive of my work. She had a large network of friends and colleagues in the Fairfield County area and did a great job of sending out emails and setting everything up. The first event was held at a new spiritual center called Finding Feathers. LJ invited mostly close friends that she knew would be supportive of me. I was actually calmer than I thought I would be.

I climbed a steep set of stairs to the meeting room where about twenty-five people were seated on folding chairs. I sat in the empty chair at the front of the room and took a deep breath. I told them my story about Ian's death, my work as an accountant and how I gave it all up to be a channeler. I then led the group on a guided meditation to help relax them and allow for any direct messages they might receive. I then opened my channel. The angels delivered a beautiful message of love to the entire group. People then began asking individual questions about money, love and health. I was surprised by the angelic humor, as well as the simple truths that were revealed. One participant asked what the angels thought of Match.com.

"Have you tried eHarmony?" they quipped back. The group laughed.

"We just couldn't resist the comeback. We don't mean to make light of it. So many people are sitting behind their desks, typing on machines, looking into a screen and hoping to find love. We do not understand why, when you are given the opportunity to come to this earth and are given a beautiful body, that you sit in isolation and pine for companionship. Those who are willing to be your companion are not sitting in the room with you. You must first go out into the world and follow your life's passion and greatest desires. You will then create the person within yourself that is most attractive to that counterpart.

"When you are participating in life, rather than complaining about it, miracles will be presented to you if only you are awake enough to be able to appreciate the gifts when they arrive. We suggest that you go out and partake in activities that feed your soul. You will then find a soul mate that fulfills your heart's greatest desire." It was such an open and loving message.

Then the next question came, like a beam of harsh light in my face. "Can you tell me about Cody?" The questioner looked to be in her late teens. Her head was shaved and she wore multiple earrings climbing up the cartilage of her ears. She had tattoos on her knuckles.

I felt a heavy weight on my chest. The energy shifted to a lower vibration; I could tell I was tapping into someone who had passed away. Although I had channeled Ian for myself, I had never channeled someone else's deceased loved one before. A flash happened before my eyes. I was picking up that he had killed himself, but I was afraid to say this, for fear of being wrong. I realized I was making it about me again. I finally asked, "Has he passed?"

"Yes." She made a sobbing sound.

Then the words burst out of me: *"I'm so sorry! I didn't mean to do it. It was a mistake!"* I was crying, filled with rage and anger. I was feeling what he must have been feeling. I broke the channel. "Did Cody kill himself?"

"Yes." More sobbing from the girl.

"Please know that I loved you. Know that I don't want you to kill yourself. I was wrong. Life is precious. I don't want you to worry about me."

"I was supposed to die too," she cried out. "Why can't I come with you?"

The angels replied through me: *"It is not your time to go. You have more work left to do on this earth. Cody needed to be taken to the other side, as his work was to continue there. We send you our love and comfort."*

I found out later that the girl had attempted suicide with her boyfriend and had been recovering in the hospital for ten days. She had been released a week earlier and was staying with my friend, Janet, who had brought her to my event.

More than two years later, I would receive an email from Janet expressing her despair and sadness that this girl had tried to kill herself again, and this time succeeded. When I read the email, a message from the other side came pouring into my head: *"There was too much chaos for her to stay, and she just couldn't pretend anymore. She is sorry to disappoint the people who tried to help her, but she is at peace and wants us to know that. She feels there was no way out but this way."*

It was sobering. Of course, I had hoped the message I had given her, two years prior, would have made everything better, but that was my ego speaking. Each person is responsible for healing himself or herself. I was just the conduit for divine guidance.

Meanwhile, I kept doing more of these types of events. Sometimes once a week, sometimes twice. The attendees seemed to enjoy the messages that were coming through. And with each event, I would discover new ways that Spirit was working with me.

At one event in Westport, Spirit began showing me things I had never seen before. As I was driving up to the house, I was consciously asking the angels and the spirits to be as obvious and helpful to me as possible. In some ways, I was growing more confident, but in other ways I was still very concerned about how people would receive me. I started the event as I did all the others, but when I looked at the first woman and closed my eyes, I saw what looked like a midnight black velvet mannequin with bright yellow hair. My eyes snapped open; I looked at the woman and closed my eyes again. The faceless mannequin reappeared. I hesitated, and said, "I'm getting a female energy with bright yellow hair."

"Oh my, God. That's my mom! She had bright yellow hair. Like a highlighter!" the guest said.

Well, that was *exactly* what I was seeing. I shared with her the message that her mother was now able to walk in heaven as she had been bedridden in her last few months on earth and that she had been reunited with her parents. I could see the relief and happiness on the daughter's face.

I then went on to read for the second person sitting in the circle. When I closed my eyes, I saw the very familiar picture of Mother Mary in my mind's eye, wearing the blue headscarf, her hands in prayer and that famous demure look downwards. I hesitantly asked the woman if she was associated with Mother Mary in any way.

"Oh, I pray to her every day. She means so much to me," she said.

At that moment, I felt another miracle had occurred. I had asked for more connection, and I had gotten it. My channel was now allowing me not only to hear messages but also to see symbols and visuals.

I continued working with these small groups of women and realized what a gift I was receiving. They helped me to grow more into the divine connector that I was brought here to be. I began to realize Spirit was preparing me to share my messages with even larger audiences. The question was—was I ready?

Although Universe felt I was, by presenting me with an offer to channel in a huge venue, I knew I was still hiding my voice from one particular person. I had always craved his approval, feeling I needed it in order to be and feel successful. And yet I wasn't being honest with him as to who I really was and what I was doing with my career. I was going to have to slay this dragon if I was ever going to win this battle for my soul. I was going to have to conquer my fear of rejection and make peace with my father.

CHAPTER 9

Since I arrived on this planet, I've struggled with feeling like I don't belong. Conceived by a man who denied my existence, adopted by a man who never wanted children, and brought up in a religion with a stern male God, I was physically and spiritually paranoid about my very existence.

Consciously or subconsciously I've spent my life grappling with all three of these father figures; or as I like to call them my "paternal trinity."

It made sense to me that I wrestled with the paternal trinity before I learned to channel divine wisdom. But once I was able to directly connect to sacred love and intelligence, I thought I would better understand how these relationships were "supposed" to work in my life.

I realized with divine connection that I was a spiritual being having a human experience. I began to understand that I agreed to these struggles with my "fathers" when I came into this lifetime. We all struggle with relationships as part of our spiritual path. The struggle helps us better understand ourselves and is part of our evolutionary process.

At different points in my life, each father caused me great angst, as well as growth in my understanding of who I was. I felt God as a child, but the feelings faded. Then I realized God was always there; I was the one who faded. Human events swayed me; it was not anything God did or didn't do.

Seeing heaven clarified for me that we are all one and that we are never separated from *The One*, unless we choose to be separate. I believe we have free will to choose our life's path. When I channel divine wisdom, so many of my clients want to be told what to do. Consistently the message I share is that Spirit is happy to help guide them on their path, but refuses to tell anyone what to do, as that is what we are here to figure out.

Organized religion is not for me. The dogma and the "rules" have done more harm than good in our society, and the divisions that have been created between different religions are unnecessary. I enjoyed the community in the various churches I was involved with for the first thirty-seven years of my life—but overall I believe in oneness and love.

I met the man whose seed created me when I was thirty. I'll never forget coming to the top of the escalator in the mall where we'd agreed to meet. I nearly fell backwards when my eyes met his face. I needed to sit down before I fainted. I had never before seen someone who looked so much like me. It was an out-of-body experience.

Once we started talking, I was thankful that he had not been part of my life. He said he never believed he was actually my father; he figured Debbie was using him as a scapegoat when she discovered she was pregnant. (Debbie was actually a virgin before meeting him that fateful night.) There was no denying our identical facial features; he knew at our meeting he was in fact my father. He also told me that he had never told his parents or his two daughters about my existence. To think that I have blood relatives who don't know of my existence is a bitter pill to swallow. Initially I struggled with the idea that if my own father didn't recognize my existence then did I really exist?

He went on to proudly explain his involvement in an extremely conservative religious movement that touted male supremacy and antigay bigotry. He had also been married a number of times, which I found ironic, given that his religion was all about the man being in charge and the woman being submissive. I guess his two prior wives weren't into that idea either. Initially I tried to maintain contact with him. Once again, my desire to be the "good girl" rather than upset him overrode my common sense. But after he made a comment to me about how I should be sure to show my son, who was three, the ultimate reverence, I cut off contact with him.

And, finally, there was my relationship with my adoptive father—the man who raised me from the time I was twelve days old.

My interactions with my father had always been distant and superficial. Our phone calls rarely went beyond surface conversations about the weather, investment strategies or the Denver Broncos, our favorite football team. We spoke in a world of permanent small talk—where things remained the most comfortable.

My dad came off as such a nice guy, and he had a great sense of humor. In social situations he was charming and witty, so most people who knew him would find it hard to believe that we were unable to communicate. Trying to get him to talk about anything deeper than the headline news was a chore. And although he was a nice man, he wasn't necessarily a good father— not a terrible father, but he was rarely able to express his love to me on any level. The closest he came was the occasional automatic response over the phone of "I love you, too," but only after I'd said it first. My brother, Eric, told me that our dad had never said "I love you" to him, and it broke my heart.

It made me wonder if he ever really loved me, or even wanted me. Deep down I think he did, or at least I *hope* he did. I believe he was emotionally crippled, maybe due to his upbringing, and he just didn't know how to be what I needed him to be. I felt that he did the absolute minimum for my brother and me, and that was it. Being adopted, I believed the man who created me didn't want me, and then growing up, I felt the man who adopted me didn't want me either. This was likely the reason that I spent my teenage and college years desperate to get approval from men, usually in ways that weren't healthy. It left me with a deep, profound wound, filled with grief.

After my parents' divorce, when I was ten, Eric and I were with my father every other weekend. Once we'd arrive at his bachelor pad, Dad would go to the main room, flip on the TV, sit in his favorite recliner, light a cigarette and pick up a paperback thriller. He'd ask us to choose a TV dinner from the freezer and to throw it in the oven for supper. My mom had always been the primary caregiver, so now that we were alone with him he was having to figure out what to do with us.

My father joined a singles' group with a couple of the other faculty members, and we started participating in more social activities, like skiing. The university had a ski lodge up in the Rocky Mountains, a small rustic cabin with a large kitchen and several bunkrooms off the living area.

On one of these ski trips, we stopped on the drive there to buy my brother and me ski outfits. I tried on several, and the sales clerk and my dad decided that I looked great in the green jacket, though I hated it. I really liked the denim one with the patchwork shoulders.

We got up to the register and as the clerk checked us out, big tears started to roll down my face. I was too scared to say anything. I felt that if I was honest, my father would abandon me, right then and there in the store. He asked me what the problem was. He was frustrated and couldn't understand why I didn't just *tell* him which one I really wanted—I couldn't explain it nor, at the time, did I even know exactly why. This feeling of mine, to do whatever my dad wanted in order to try to gain his love, would be a constant theme throughout my life.

These visits lasted until Eric and I moved with our mom and her second husband, Gary, to Wisconsin when I was twelve. That same year, when we went back to Denver for Thanksgiving, my dad married Karen. She looked exactly like Kate Jackson, the brunette from the TV show *Charlie's Angels*. Karen was a divorcée with a high-powered finance job. She had an eight-year old son, Shane, whose father lived in Alaska. I never warmed up to Karen, finding her to be demanding and controlling of my father.

It appeared to me that she had married my father so he could raise her son. My dad's professor schedule allowed a tremendous amount of flexibility, so he seemed to be always taking Shane to orthodontic appointments or picking him up from lacrosse practice while Karen worked her full-time corporate job. Apparently, Karen and my dad were planning on only living together and not getting married. I learned many years later that his parents told him that if he didn't marry Karen since they were living together, they would cut him out of their will. My grandparents also made it clear that they did not want one dime of their inheritance to go to either Karen or Shane.

On one of our summer visits, my Dad, Karen, Shane, Eric and I went to one of their friend's homes for a barbecue. While there I asked Karen if I could borrow the keys from her purse to get a sweatshirt from the car. I immediately returned the keys to her bag when I came back into the house.

After driving back to our father's house later that night, Karen couldn't find the key ring that had both the extra car key and the only house key in her bag. She began screaming at me, saying that I had deliberately not put them back in her purse. I was terrified—I *knew* that I had returned them. My father was silent. After about forty-five minutes of a hysterical Karen berating me, my dad found them under her car seat. Apparently her purse fell backwards, and the keys fell out. Neither of them apologized. They just walked into the house and went to their bedroom. I could hear Karen in their room continuing to disparage me; not once did my father defend me. Nor did he ever bring the incident up again. I was devastated.

As the years went by, our time together felt forced, inauthentic and nothing but obligatory. We never had any conversations that had any deep meaning or even an inkling of his philosophy on life other than how important it was to get a respectable job with benefits and to make a lot of money. He always emphasized that it was impolite to discuss money or your desire to want it or have it, yet he spent countless hours keeping track of his growing stock portfolio and retirement funds—almost to the point of obsession. It was clear that my dad had a love/hate relationship with money, like he was fighting with an entity that was separate from him. It was weird.

It wasn't until I was a senior in high school, when I had graduated a semester early and gone to Japan to visit my aunt and uncle, that I was told that my grandparents "had money." I was flabbergasted. I still wasn't sure what the actual dollar amount was, except that my aunt alluded to it being over a million. *They were*

millionaires! What? Where had I been all these years?
How could I be related to millionaires? I started to think
back to my visits to their home in Shenandoah, Iowa.
They did live on one of the grandest streets in town, in a
meticulously maintained elegant house, albeit modest by
today's standards. Grandpa did own his own golf cart,
and they did purchase a new Buick every two years. I
also remembered my Grandmother had a rather sizeable
diamond ring. They certainly weren't flaunting their
wealth, but then again they lived in a very small
conservative town. These traditional Midwestern values
were how my father was raised and taught to deal with
money. This may have been why he refused to openly
discuss it.

When I was eighteen, just before I left for Japan
to visit my aunt and uncle who were teaching at Nanzan
University in Nagoya, Gary, my stepdad, threw me out of
the house in Minnesota. I'd been a cashier at the local
grocery store since I'd turned sixteen, because once I
turned the legal working age, my stepfather refused to
pay for any of my expenses, including school lunches. I
would be using all of my own money to make the trip.

One day before leaving, I was talking on the
phone in the kitchen to a friend. Gary was in the adjacent
room resting on the couch. He told me to lower my voice
or get off the phone. Given that the phone was attached to
the wall, I told him that if he wanted to nap during the
day, he could go to his bedroom. I was eighteen and this
was one of the first times I used my voice to speak up for
myself. He jumped off the couch and started shouting.
My mom arrived on the scene and with all the fury he
could muster, he said, "Either she goes, or I go!" My
mom was crying. Knowing she was stuck between a rock
and a hard place, I told her I would go. So much for using
my voice….

After returning from Japan, I moved to Denver to live with my Dad and Karen. I would be attending Denver University in the fall, so moving there a few months before I had planned was not a problem. That August my grandparents took all of us (my dad, Karen, Shane, Eric and me along with my aunt, her husband and two kids) to the island of Kauai, Hawaii, to celebrate their fiftieth wedding anniversary. Now that I was tipped off to their situation, it became pretty obvious that they had money.

In college my dad suggested I study international relations with a focus on Japan. The plan was to become an international business executive who spoke Japanese. Who was I to protest? I didn't have an opinion, because I didn't know I was capable of having one. I thought life was about doing what you were told, as it made people happy when you did and not happy when you didn't. I liked people being happy. My dad was always excited when he would talk to me about these plans, so I just fed off of his enthusiasm. It felt like he was living vicariously through me. He had never had the opportunity to study abroad, so he was determined that I would. I had no desire to go to school in another country, and even if I had, I don't know if it would have been Japan—that just happened to be where my Aunt Linda (my dad's sister) had studied.

In order to attend the year abroad in Japan, I first had to complete an intensive Japanese language program at Middlebury College in Vermont, where my aunt was now a professor. The rules were, after two weeks, we weren't allowed to speak anything but Japanese. This is when I first realized I had a major problem. My higher self finally woke up and began a full-scale protest. I hated the program. Panic ensued. I literally wanted to kill myself, and contemplated throwing myself off the bridge into the river that ran through town. Visiting for six weeks was fun, and in retrospect also my dad's idea—but living and studying there for a year? It was worse when I realized if I quit my father would lose a lot of money because of me.

Finally, I confessed my misgivings to my aunt. She was extremely supportive and intervened by talking to my father. I left the program a week later, with dread and humiliation in my heart.

I was at this point slowly realizing that I had a voice, but I was terrified to use it. I felt broken as a child, and I felt I had no right to be myself, no right to express what I really wanted.

My father was disappointed but not angry. When I got back to Colorado, he suggested that I get an accounting degree. I immediately complied. Apparently I had not learned anything, as I so readily agreed to follow his advice once again. I'm sure I was trying to make up for all the trouble I'd caused. In order to graduate on time, I needed to take a few summer classes. Fortunately, I thrived in the accounting department, and the last two years in college were pretty uneventful. I was even one of the few graduates who landed a lucrative corporate job, with great benefits, in San Francisco. For years, Dad promised to take me anywhere I wanted to go in the world when I graduated college. Even though we'd often have long discussions about where we'd go, he instead gave me a toolbox.

Just after I graduated in 1989, I learned my mom and my dad were each divorcing their second spouses. I was told that Karen was having an affair with her much younger male assistant, and Gary was having an affair with *his* assistant at the Lutheran corporate offices in Chicago. It was shocking and yet a relief, as both of my relationships with my parents' spouses had been tumultuous. After the divorces, I never spoke to or saw Karen or Gary again.

I was working at Price Waterhouse in San Francisco in accounting. My brother would call and tell me how dad would show up at his door, his face streaked with tears, and then sit on his couch and talk about all his problems in painstaking detail. He had a second failed marriage; this time *he* was the one who was betrayed. He told Eric he was getting counseling and even confessed his remorse for not being a better father. He would lament that he wished he had been more demonstrative with his love. He was confused and adrift with this overwhelming sense of grief for the loss of time and things that he would never get back.

Slowly my dad returned to his usual ways of remoteness and isolation. He had left the university and had become the chief operating officer at the Denver Zoo. Here he found his true passion and his desires fulfilled. His love of travel, photography and organization was evident in this position; he quite visibly came to life.

He traveled to Africa at least a dozen times, often leading groups and sharing his passion for wildlife, conservation and animal photography. During this time my dad would proudly show me his balance sheet, so I could see his net worth. I didn't know what the appropriate response should be, especially since he had always warned me never to discuss money. I was happy for him, and yet wondered why he rarely spent any of his money on himself or others. *What is the point of accumulating wealth if you aren't going to use it for anything?*

****

My dad met his third wife, Cyndy, in the zoo world. Twenty years my dad's junior, she was working at the Omaha Zoo, was divorced, and had no kids. He kept this relationship quiet at the beginning. I think he was being cautious given his past relationship record. They dated long distance for many years, and ultimately got married in Africa without inviting any family.

I saw my Dad only once every two or three years, when I would come back to visit him and my brother in Denver. He rarely, if ever, came to visit me. Though he had plenty of room in his house in Denver, I never stayed there. His smoking drove me insane. I couldn't breathe, even though he said he only smoked outside. Because he couldn't smell it, he thought it didn't stink. Growing up with his smoking and then not being around it for many years made it hard for me to be around cigarette smoke.

When I was forty, he finally took me on that promised college graduation trip. It was actually a family trip to Kenya which included my family and my brother's family. Africa was my dad's favorite place in the world. He wanted to give us the ultimate Kenyan experience. We stayed in five-star accommodations and took private planes to three different areas. It was amazing, but terrifying.

Of course we witnessed the animals in the wild— which were spectacular; however, due to my father's connections we also did some not so common activities. We fed a baby rhino orphaned by poachers. A tour was arranged at a Masai village, where we danced with the tribe and handed out baseball caps to the kids. We also discussed the ideas behind female genital mutilation at puberty with our guides, which was quite a discussion.

It was obvious that traveling to Africa with his family brought pleasure to my father beyond anything I had ever seen. As we celebrated New Year's Eve at an elephant tent camp under the stars, I had never seen my father happier. At that moment, he was living his ultimate dream. There is a picture of all of us, just before the celebrations—my dad sitting in the middle of his family, all of us dressed in safari garb, him beaming with joy.

Due to the extreme differences in culture, as well as the rising tensions in that country (and my sensitivity to energy and emotions) I found it nearly impossible to enjoy myself. Within months of our return, violence erupted and swept the city of Nairobi, leaving thousands dead. The trip itself was well worth doing, but also a haunting experience that stayed with me long after I left.

****

Two years later, when my family had flown from Connecticut to Denver for Christmas in 2008, my dad talked to my brother and me about his estate plans. He explained that he wanted our input. He was basically leaving everything to Cyndy in a family trust. He explained how he felt obligated to financially take care of Cyndy, as she had left her full-time job when they had married. He also told us he didn't want to give her any money outright, as he was concerned she'd spend *his* fortune on her next husband.

I had serious issues with this plan. It was difficult to discuss these matters with my dad as money was such a taboo issue, and yet he had asked for our opinion. I would churn the different machinations of the ways he could restructure his estate plans over and over in my head until I felt I had to express my concerns to him before I internally exploded—usually about once a year. After I had expressed myself, I would be able to let the feelings go for a while, until they began to build again. It almost felt like a demon or wild animal inside of me. As soon as I'd begin to give it some space, it would grow and grow until I had to let it out. My dad would quietly listen to whatever I said and tell me he'd think about it. He'd often say he'd talk to a lawyer, but I was never sure he actually did so. He was the king of the non-confrontational conversation shuffle, and he would steer the discussion to some investment strategy he'd been researching or to the weather.

I had never thought of myself as money hungry, but I was surprised how petty and concerned I became over the details of my father's will. I hated the person that I allowed it to make me. I emphatically didn't want my grandparents' money going into the family trust. My grandmother was still alive at age one hundred, with total dementia, and my father was in charge of her finances. For me, the money would be proof that I belonged to *this* family, as typically family money gets passed down from one generation to the next—and not to the third wife. Once again the deep seeds of my adoption would push to the surface to feed my insecurities. Also, I was adamant that I didn't want to be tied to Cyndy for the rest of our lives as co-trustees of a family trust. We didn't have much of a relationship while my Dad was alive; why would I want to continue a relationship with her— especially purely a financial one, in which I'm having to help make decisions about how best to provide for her by using the monetary resources provided for by my grandparents—once my father passed?

Despite my objections, and my father's continued assurances that he was "thinking about how best to restructure it" he never changed his will. After three years of back and forth discussions, I'd had enough. I'd been doing my own healing, and was beginning to realize that the money was a carrot, and that I was hiding who I was to be able some day to get that carrot. My father knew I quit my accounting job, but he had no idea I was on such a deep spiritual path and that I was a channel of divine wisdom now. I felt I had to tell him who I was, and let the money be damned. The whole thing was a tangle of who I was, who I wanted to be, and what the money was making me.

In November of 2011, I flew to Denver to talk to my father. I thought he would disown me. He had designs on me being a corporate CFO, but I had decided that talking to angels was a better career path. *Even I was skeptical* of the idea. Just saying it aloud to myself made me terrified of his reaction. I also realized that the reason the money mattered so much to me was because my father raised me to believe that it *should*. Until you are aware of *why* you believe in certain ideas, you just take them as truth, rather than wondering how you came to them.

My brother Eric and I had been on a similar spiritual path, and also wanted to discuss the estate plan with Dad. He agreed to tell him that we ultimately didn't care what he did, but we did not want to be tied to a long-term trust that forced us to interact with Cyndy for years to come. We felt it wasn't fair to us, and it wasn't fair to her.

My brother and I sat across the table from my father at a breakfast diner. The place was packed, and platters of pancakes and waffles were being served all around us.

"Dad," I braced myself. Tears began to fall from my eyes. "I have something to say to you."

He stared at me and rubbed his thumb across his forefinger and middle finger together, a habit that he did when he really wanted a cigarette.

"I feel as though I've had to portray this perfect person to you my entire life to get your approval. I've felt as though you've held our grandparents' money out there as a reward and that I'd only get it if I was who you wanted me to be. Well, I'm done; I'm not going to lie by omission any longer. I, I... talk to angels, and spirits, and I never told you because I was afraid of what you would think."

My nose began to run, and my heart was pounding in my chest. "Take me or leave me, but I just can't be silent any longer, and if I don't get the money, then so be it." I noticed a few people looking at our table, as my voice had gotten louder and louder.

My dad stared at me, still rubbing his fingers. He had no expression and no response.

My brother then explained that he felt as though his desire to become a fine artist was never enough for my father and that he too was done trying to please him.

"I really don't understand where all this is coming from," my dad said, visibly angry. "I'm trying to lock this money up, into a trust, so I can take care of Cyndy. I don't understand how you think I don't approve of you. I brag about each of you to everyone I know." He looked first at me and then at my brother.

"But Dad, how are you bragging about me? What are you telling them? That I'm a CPA with Price Waterhouse? I quit that job almost 20 years ago! Or what, that I run my own business—do you even *know* what my business is? No, Dad, you don't. You've never even asked me! And no, I don't know that you brag about me, or what you even brag about because I have never heard you tell *me* that you are proud of me."

As hard as that conversation was, it was necessary and beyond overdue. As the words left my mouth, I felt free—I had come out of hiding. I spoke my truth and felt victorious! Over the next few months I was open with him about my speaking engagements and would call him on my way home after a group event and share my excitement with him. He occasionally would make a comment of encouragement, like some public-speaking tips, but he never asked me any direct questions about why or how I channeled the angels and other spirits. But, at least, I'd been honest and the curtain was lifted. At least he met me on some common ground. It wasn't

143

exactly what I had always wanted, but it was something, and after so much time without any real personal connection with my dad, I was grateful for it.

He also told my brother and me that he'd work on a new plan for his will. My grandmother had recently passed away at 103. He was in the process of sorting out her estate and said that he needed to address our concerns. I was honored and thrilled to receive my grandmother's two-carat diamond ring. For the first time in my life, I felt like everything was going right for me.

CHAPTER 10

The Ridgefield Playhouse is the beautifully renovated former auditorium of an old high school. The five-hundred-seat venue in our small town in Connecticut has had many star performers: Peter Yarrow, Marcel Marceau, Joan Baez, The Bacon Brothers, Michael Feinstein, Clint Black, The Doobie Brothers, Brian Wilson, and many more. Given that the original high school was built in 1938 (and in use until the mid-1970's), the interior is quite ornate. There is a marquee entrance into a spacious lobby where they sell drinks, popcorn and candy. Two staircases from the lobby lead to a balcony. The main auditorium is filled with the typical theater-style red seats. This night was to be my first spiritual mediumship performance on a stage, and I was ready for it.

It took a great deal of preparation. Six months earlier, I had begun working with a speaking coach to formulate an engaging presentation. I had also worked with a professional sound producer to create a CD, *The Essential Being Meditations*, to sell at the event. A lot was riding on this; I sensed that my entire career as a spiritual teacher would be determined by the outcome.

Working with Spirit requires elements of trust and faith. I was extremely nervous that night, overly concerned with trying to prove what I could do during my performance. Obviously, there was no guarantee that anything would happen; I just needed to have faith and literally go with the flow.

I went back to the "green room," nothing more than a small dressing room, to change into my performance outfit, which I had debated over for months. I settled on white jeans with angel wings embroidered on the back pockets and a lavender colored western-style cowboy shirt I had purchased in Key West. Soon enough, I was standing in the wings of the auditorium being introduced by Allison, the Playhouse director.

As usual, Allison came out on stage before the performance to welcome the audience. I had attended many events at the venue and was familiar with her process. Dressed like a motorcycle babe with black leather pants and a studded leather vest that exposed a well-toned tummy, and with her messy mane of long blond hair, Allison's presence was wild and striking.

My speech coach had given me specific instructions to write out my introduction and give it to Allison ahead of time, which I did. To my horror, not only did Allison not read my introduction, she said casually: "Tonight we have Lisa Jones." She paused and looked over at me standing just offstage. "I'm not really sure what she does. I met her in the lobby of The Playhouse when Gabrielle Bernstein was here last time. What was it you were doing in the lobby? Reading cards or something, right?"

I was struck dumb. I worried she was belittling me and sending a message to the audience that I was nothing but a sideshow card-reader. Could she really not remember why she had offered me this opportunity?

"Uh, yeah..." I awkwardly replied.

It felt like being thrown in with sharks and forced to swim. For good or bad, that was my introduction—as inauspicious as it was. I had no choice but to walk on stage and begin the evening. There were about 140 people, mostly women, sitting attentively. Most of them were in the center, with a few scattered in the left and right sections. The spotlight in my face made it hard to see, but I don't think there was anyone in the balcony.

I started off by telling my life story. I wanted to give an overview of how I came to acquire my skill of being able to talk to angels and other spirits. I was so nervous that I couldn't seem to stop myself from telling them *everything* and ended up telling them far too much, partly out of nervousness and partly out of a desire to open myself up before we began.

I told them things I rarely told anyone, about being molested as a four year old by a female babysitter, about losing my virginity to date rape at fifteen, about how I got a fractured skull when my college boyfriend pushed me out of a moving car during a fight over who would pay for breakfast.

I told them how the 1989 World Series earthquake had brought Ian and me together and how two years later, on the day he proposed marriage, three thousand homes burned down in Oakland, one of which nearly was his house.

I went on to explain the rest of the sorrows and blessings I'd experienced in my life. This was not for the sake of pity or to merely expose my dirty laundry, but as a way of sharing the idea that we all go through stuff— good and bad. Somehow I felt that if people knew my deepest, darkest secrets and then saw how happy I was, that they could see hope for themselves too. I felt nothing was so dark, scary or sad that shining the beautiful light of Spirit on it couldn't fix it. I wanted the audience to see that each and every event made us the people we are today. Though I began speaking out of nervousness, when I finished, I realized that part of me knew exactly what I was doing. And Spirit had guided me.

I then led the audience on a healing meditation. Michael James, an extremely talented musician who I had recently been introduced to, graciously agreed to accompany me on keyboard and guitar, playing spiritually-inspired music. Between the music and the angels guiding me, the meditation was a huge success. But then came the third part of the evening: the channeling. Things would not go so smoothly.

I stood out there and tried to channel but nothing happened. I mean, *nothing.* I didn't panic; I didn't run away—I just stepped forward. This book begins with this moment because it is central to understanding my journey—and by extension, everyone's journey. It comes with that decision to step forward.

I opened my eyes and calmly stood up. "Well, you never can predict what Spirit will do. I've called in the angels, and they don't seem to be interested in coming through for me right now. Instead, I'd like to ask for a volunteer to come up on stage, and I can demonstrate for you how I conduct a private session—but I'll do it in front of a live audience."

I figured I'd be hard pressed to get anyone to raise his or her hand. In fact, I had talked to my speaking coach ahead of time, and we had discussed the options if something were to go really badly. We were now in that nightmare scenario, but I would not let it defeat me. My coach assured me his wife had agreed to raise her hand if and when I needed any volunteers.

I looked out at the audience. I had noticed where Don and his wife were sitting earlier and to my shock, she was not raising her hand! As my heart took another giant leap toward exiting my body, I shielded my eyes from the spotlight and the sharp glare dissolved. Half of the crowd had their hands up! My eyes were drawn to the front right; I pointed at someone, and she practically jumped out of her seat and onto the stage.

She came straight over to me. "I'm so excited. My friend follows you on Twitter, and so we came to see you and now here I am!"

"Wow, Twitter. Awesome." I was intrigued that someone from Twitter actually came to my event, still mystified by the phenomenon of social media. "So tell me your name."

"I'm Carolyn."

"Hi Carolyn, welcome. Okay, so I'm going to say a little invocation, and then I usually pull three cards." I stopped. "Oh wait, I don't have my cards out here—you know I wasn't planning on doing this."

Over the loudspeaker came a voice. "Lisa, where are your cards? I'll get them for you." It was Allison. "Tell me where they are. I'll go get them."

"Oh, thanks!" I looked out into the crowd, trying to see where Allison was standing. "They're in the dressing room, on the shelf next to the mirror." I was surprised by Allison's offer of help, especially considering the way she had introduced me. I'm not sure what turned her around; maybe it was pity for me being stranded out there or maybe she trusted I was the real thing, since I wasn't pretending to contact Spirit just to make it through this.

As we waited for Allison and my cards, Carolyn and I chatted. She was a petite woman in her mid-30s from New York. A newly single mom of two young boys, Carolyn was happy to be out of the house for a change of pace. "Am I supposed to tell you what happened?"

"Feel free to share with me what you'd like."

Many people think that they shouldn't tell a psychic anything in order to "test" them—as if it were a trick or a challenge of some kind. This is adversarial and exactly the thing that hinders readings. It turns into a self-fulfilling prophecy: If you don't believe, you create an environment that won't be able to change your mind.

I have always found that I am able to get a much faster, stronger connection to Spirit when the person I'm reading for is open, honest and forthcoming with important information. Without information, Spirit will sometimes talk about things that the person isn't really interested in. Sometimes if they do not ask specifically to connect with someone, for example, their deceased father, a great aunt will come through because she has a stronger connection than the father.

This testing approach hurts the process, which is fitting in a way: Those that don't really believe don't get a strong reading. The belief is almost a prerequisite. This is why it's called a leap of faith. Overall, I feel I do my best work when I have at least a general direction.

"Well, I lost my husband, not long ago," she said.

"Oh, Carolyn, I'm so sorry."

Allison walked on stage and handed me the deck of cards. "Oh, thank you." She also gave Carolyn a handheld microphone.

I shuffled the deck and had her pick three cards, face down. The first card had the word *Passion* on it.

"Well, the first card is her blockage card. And that's passion." I said as I looked into the audience. "So right now there's a lack of passion in your life..."

"That's funny, because that's the card I picked out there." She pointed to the lobby of the theater. "Before you walked in, there was a table with a stack of your business cards—you know, how you have different words on the back of each one? My friend said, 'Close your eyes and pick a card.' And the card I picked was Passion. I said to my other friend, '*That's* what I'm lacking in.'" The audience reacted with a small wave of laughter.

"Wow! That's confirmation," I said.

I turned over the middle card, which represents what a person needs to do to heal the blockage. The word was *Gratitude*. I told her that by being grateful for the fact that she was still here on Earth and that she had two beautiful boys to take care of, she would soon see the passion of her life start to bloom.

I then turned over the final outcome card, *Sanctuary*. I told Carolyn that she must have more gratitude in her life to heal the blockage of passion. Then she will ultimately end up with a beautiful place that she can call her sanctuary. I could imagine that after her husband's death her home was not exactly a place that made her feel safe and secure. I went through something similar with Ian and my old house.

"That's interesting," she said. "I just started sleeping in my bedroom again; it's been a year and a half since he died."

"Well, please allow this to be a confirmation that you deserve a beautiful sanctuary to help heal your soul."

I picked up the Calling All Angels bottle and nodded toward Carolyn. "Okay, if you're ready," I said, to get her approval to spray the essential oils over the top of her head. She nodded. "Excellent. I'll take another spritz of this myself." I lifted my left arm and sprayed my armpit. The audience roared with laughter. I set the bottle down. "If it's okay with you, I'm going to place my hands on your shoulders and then I'll open my channel, and we'll see what comes through."

"I'm ready."

I closed my eyes. "I call on God, Universe, angels, Archangel Michael. Please stand behind us for protection and love. Archangel Raphael, stand to our left for healing and sanctuary. This time I call on Archangel Haniel, for grace and comfort and love."

Long pause. I felt tingling at the top of my head at my crown chakra. My head began to bob forward and back. Just before I start getting messages I feel a connection take place, like an electrical cord plugging into a wall socket. "Yes, Carolyn, we are with you. We are your angels." My voice was deep and deliberate. "The name Richard is coming to me."

It's very difficult to explain how I receive the information. The best way to describe it is to say that it's just a *knowing*. It was as though the name *Richard* just showed up in my brain. I didn't hear it; I didn't see it; it just suddenly *appeared*. I guess that is what the channel is, a direct connection to spirit. It delivers the information without me having to do anything.

"Yes, that's my father. But he's still alive."

I discovered through my work that not only could I connect with people who have passed on, but I could also connect to people who were still alive. It was usually because they had something on a soul level to express to the person in front of me.

"Your father is concerned for you. He wants you to know that he is here for you and happy to help you in any way you need."

"Oh, yes. That sounds like my dad—thank you."

"Now the name, *Joseph*." From the audience, where Carolyn had been sitting, there was a sudden commotion. I wasn't sure if it was gasps from her friends or a suppressed yelp.

"Oh my God. Yes. That was my husband's name. Joe." Carolyn became emotional. Tears began to flow down her face.

"I'm getting a lot of pressure on my chest. Did he die of a heart attack?"

"Yes," Carolyn said.

"I'm seeing him lying on the floor in a hallway in front of…it looks like a bedroom door."

"Oh, my god, yes, that's where he collapsed and died. That's why I can't go into my bedroom!"

The audience gasped.

"Joe wants you to know that he is coming to you with grace and love. Can you feel the energy flowing through my hands into your being?"

She nodded.

"He's so proud of you. He's talking about leaving a window open. He feels like he can be closer to you when you leave the window open and when you look out into the back garden. He's telling you, 'Thank you, thank you, thank you.' You are such an amazing role model. He couldn't have asked for anyone better to raise his two boys. He wants you to move forward. Don't be sad for him. He's fine. He just wants you to be fine. Are you moving or maybe traveling to Florida?"

"Oh my goodness. My sister is planning a trip for us all to go to Florida next year!"

"He's saying, 'Do, it, do it.' He wants you to move forward. He wants you to be happy and find another love in your life. Are you seeing someone now?"

"I got hit on at the bar the other night." Laughter erupted from the audience.

"Joe wants you to know that meeting and falling in love with someone else does not mean that you are forgetting about him or that you are betraying him in any way. Since we are all one already, inviting another soul into your life expands the circle of love. You have all of eternity to reunite with and share the love of all those you have loved on the earth plane. I'm feeling the energy begin to pull back. I think that's all we are going to get from Joe today."

Carolyn seemed overwhelmed, but happy. "That helps me more than you will ever know. I just have to tell you: A friend of mine sees things in her dreams. Since my husband died she has had a recurring dream at 3 a.m., which is the time that Joe died. He's telling her to tell me to leave the window open. So that is amazing that you said that just now, because I didn't understand why he wanted me to do that. I really can't thank you enough." Carolyn got up and gave me a big hug.

"Let's give Carolyn a big hand for being brave enough to come up here on stage," I said.

As the audience was clapping, I was worried about bringing another person up on stage. I was afraid that I'd be pushing my luck if I chose another one. Before I could give it any more thought, I saw all the hands go up again. I chose someone from the third row.

Sandy looked to be in her late thirties and had loosely curled, shoulder-length blond hair. She was tall, wearing jeans and a casual top. She quickly sat down in the director's chair and told me that her fourteen-year-old daughter had passed about six weeks earlier from medical complications. I was the third psychic that she had come to see. She was desperate to connect.

I told her that I saw a big number twenty-four and the letter J. "My daughter's name is Jessica. That was the number on her soccer jersey." The audience again gasped.

I was getting the name Elisa, which I thought couldn't be right, so I asked about Elisa or Melissa, just to cover my bases.

"Elisa is my eleven-year-old daughter."

I nodded. "Well, I'm getting a very strong message from Elisa. It's sweet. She is saying, 'Mommy, I'm still here. Please don't forget me. I know you are in tremendous pain because Jessica died, but please don't forget that I still need you here and now."

I turned to Sandy and said, "She asked me to share that message with you because she isn't able to say that to you face to face."

Sandy blinked. "I know she's still here. Are you getting anything from Jessica?" Sandy just couldn't hear such a beautiful message from her living daughter.

"No, nothing else." I realized then and there that no matter what else I told her, nothing was going to ease her pain. The grief was too strong, and she was desperately grasping for answers that would never fill the hole in her heart.

From my own experience of losing my husband, I found that nothing anyone could have told me in the weeks just after his death could have healed my wounds. In the initial weeks after Ian's death, friends, neighbors and relatives rallied around the children and me. It was the time *after* that when I thought I wouldn't be able to survive. I referred to it as "no man's land," a time when everyone around seemed afraid to approach to offer support, and I was incapable of reaching out to them. This was where Sandy was in her grief. It was best to let her go back and sit in the audience.

After Sandy left I decided to ask for questions from the audience. Allison gave the microphone to the woman closest to her who was raising her hand.

"I have a question about signs." A smartly dressed woman with short salt-and-pepper hair stood up. "Can you talk about how to tell if you are getting a sign from your angels or even from someone who has passed?"

"Excellent question. The way that you can tell if you are getting a sign from Spirit is simple: *Just ask.* The exciting news is that Spirit is sending us multiple messages every single day. Unfortunately, we just usually aren't awake enough to realize it, let alone to be able to interpret what the sign means.

I've found the best way to see a sign is to ask your angels or your loved one to show you a specific sign, and then be on the lookout. It may take you a few days to realize what the sign is, but once you start looking, you'll begin to see a pattern, like feathers, or pennies, or butterflies. The key is to be open to seeing everything around you until you can identify what Spirit is consistently showing you. Then, once you know what your sign is, it's easy to see when Spirit is trying to communicate with you or if you are simply looking for validation." I told them that my sign for Ian had always been a dragonfly.

"When Ian was getting cancer treatment in Seattle, the kids and I flew to Minnesota for a few days to attend my mother's wedding. While we were visiting our lake house, dragonflies were everywhere. The kids were seven and nine and weren't happy with these big bugs buzzing their heads and even landing on the top of them. They screamed and dove underwater to get the dragonflies off of their heads. I was worried that they would panic, thrash around and hurt themselves, so I told them that the dragonflies were angels and that if they landed on their heads it was good luck. That changed the whole situation.

Suddenly they were competing to see how many dragonflies they could get to land on their heads. Well, after Ian died, six months later, we started noticing dragonflies flitting about almost everywhere, and I wondered if this was a sign for us. I then asked him to be very clear about letting me know that he was still with us. Then I began to see that not only were there lots of dragonflies wherever we went, but typically there would be one beautiful dragonfly that would fly up to either Jenna or Rob and circle their head and then buzz by me and soar off into the distance.

This would happen at soccer games, dance recitals, going in and out of the grocery store, walking in New York City. It was so comforting, as it was a great reminder that even though Ian had passed away, he still made his presence known to us on a regular basis."

The microphone was then handed to a woman who was sitting about six rows back. She was slender with thick auburn hair, styled in a bob. "I don't have a question, but I just have to share my experience of coming here tonight. I was all dressed and ready to leave my house. In fact, I had already gotten into my car and backed it out of the garage. Then an overwhelming feeling overcame me—it sounds so crazy, but I felt that I needed to add a broach to my jacket. I'm telling you, it was a really strong feeling! I'm a jewelry designer, and I created a broach about a year ago that I had never worn before. So I went back inside, into my room where I keep my jewelry box and added this broach to my jacket." She pointed to the lapel where her hand had been over her heart.

"It's a dragonfly! Can you believe this? I can't believe this. After your story about your sign being a dragonfly, and then here I am with this dragonfly broach. I mean, why was I possessed to go and put this on? Your story and then how I ended up here with this dragonfly on me. Wow."

The audience broke into spontaneous applause. I put my hand to my heart and felt a wave of love wash through me. "Thank you so much for sharing your story. This is why I do what I do. This story is a great example of the types of events that are right in front of us each and every day. The real art of living happy is waking up to Spirit and allowing yourself to be more aware of what is happening to you *right now*."

I took a breath and looked out into the crowd. "I hope you enjoyed the evening and understand a little bit more about the art of living happy."

The audience broke into applause. I waved and walked off stage. It was an exhilarating evening, and one I will cherish forever.

****

As I walked through the lobby after the show, my friends Terri and Peter ran up to me excitedly.

"Ian was in the audience!" Terri exclaimed. They both seemed out of breath. "I was five rows back from Peter and afterwards I asked him, 'Who was that guy sitting next to you?' Peter says, 'Nobody was sitting next to me. What are you talking about?'"

"I described the guy. Brown hair, broad shoulders, a little taller than him and... oh my God."

Peter interrupted. "I knew it was Ian. Because before I even came tonight, I had the weirdest thing happen. I wasn't planning on coming, but I felt someone firmly tap my shoulder. I turned to look, but no one was there. Then I heard, 'Go to the event.' I shook my head, because I really thought I was losing it. Then I heard it again, 'Go to the event.' I grabbed my car keys and drove straight here. Without a doubt, I know it was Ian."

After all the excitement died down, I wanted to celebrate but everyone needed to go home. However, David made up for the lack of other people. He was so enthusiastic and supportive. I had never seen him so animated and excited about anything that I had done before. We talked about each moment of the night and what he liked best and what parts that I could improve upon. It was exactly what I needed.

Later that night, I talked to my daughter. She told me she couldn't believe that I was channeling names and that I actually said them aloud. "I was sitting in my seat, and as soon as you said the first name, I think it was Richard, I cringed. I was so worried that you would get the names wrong. But I have to say I was impressed—the angels really came through for you!"

A week or so later, while walking down Main Street, I ran into someone who had attended the event.

"Oh Lisa! I just have to thank you so much for your amazing show the other night. I was so moved by everything you said and especially by the meditation that you did before you brought those people up on stage. Lisa, I have blocked tear ducts." She gently grabbed hold of my left arm and lowered her voice. "Which means I don't have tears. I haven't had a tear run down my face in over ten years." She released my arm, took a step back and became much more animated. "During your meditation, tears were streaming, flowing down my face. How is that possible? It was a miracle, a true miracle."

"Thank you for sharing your story. I'm so happy you were able to attend the show, but I can't take any credit for the tears or the miracle. That was all Spirit and you working together. Again, thank you for telling me this. I love hearing these stories."

Another woman, Sharon, called me and asked if we could get together and have lunch. She had been diagnosed with lymphoma a few years earlier and could really relate to my story about Ian. Although she was cured by the cancer treatments three months later, she ended up in a coma. The treatments were too hard on her delicate system, so some of her organs shut down. She was in a coma for almost eight weeks. She told me some of the stories and experiences she had while she was in the coma. It was amazing.

The main reason she wanted to have lunch was to share with me how my story helped her husband come to terms with what he had seen in the hospital room while she was in her coma. He had never been a believer in any types of spirits or even an afterlife. However, after coming and listening to my story of learning to talk to angels, then being shown heaven and ultimately bringing messages of people who have passed on right there on stage, he had a complete change of heart. Her husband had witnessed shadowy entities floating around the hospital room and before my event he had dismissed them as a figment of his imagination. She thanked me for sharing my story as it validated what she had experienced in her coma and what her husband had experienced.

It was like a dam had broken and the rush of water just couldn't be stopped. Another person got in touch with me to tell me she saw angels standing behind me with their hands on my shoulders and then even bigger angels standing behind those angels. She also saw a spirit that I think was my friend Michael. Whenever I hesitated or began to go quiet, she said he would walk over and put his hand on my arm, and then instantly I would come up with some excellent bit of information. If he didn't have his hand on my arm, he was walking back and forth on the stage looking out and waving to people, which would be totally something Michael would do.

After the event, I spent days and then weeks just waiting for something big to happen. I had received a call from a friend who knew someone in Los Angeles who wanted to see a video of the evening, and there was talk about a possible reality TV show. I knew it! I knew something big would happen.

And then...nothing. I sent the video, and there was some back and forth communication, but nothing came of it. I thought I'd get more bookings for larger venues or at least more clients. None of that happened.

Instead the worst thing happened.

Again.

CHAPTER 11

In July of 2012, Jenna and I were packing for a mother-daughter high school graduation trip to Europe. Every year, the kids and I made a trip to Minnesota to visit my mom's lake cabin. Because of David's work schedule, I typically took the kids to Minnesota by myself. That year Rob would be going to Boy Scout camp, so it would just be Jenna and me.

Jenna asked if we could go somewhere other than Minnesota. "Maybe Spain? We could visit David's sister. Doesn't she have a place there?"

Louise, and her husband Alan, had a beautiful home in Malaga. They would take their two daughters, Jordan and Ana, there each summer to ensure a warmer experience than they would have in Ireland. Once we had the okay for a visit, we decided to extend our trip to include more of Europe, including stops in Barcelona, Aix-en-Provence and Paris.

The grief over Jenna leaving for college was so deep that I could hardly put it into words. She was going to school 1,400 miles away. She'd graduated on what would have been my twentieth wedding anniversary to Ian. Her impending absence also felt like a death to me, and reminded me of losing her father. I was happy for her, excited for her new life, but the heartache was profound.

While we were packing, I received a phone call.

"Hi Lisa. It's Dad." I'm not sure why he always had to clarify that for me.

"Hey Dad! How are you? Jenna and I are so excited. I can't thank you enough for all your help in planning our trip." He had given us a bunch of language books, maps, and guidebooks.

"Oh good. I'm not sure how relevant those twenty-year-old guidebooks will be, but I'm glad I could pass them along...."

I sensed he wanted to say something. "Anyway, Cyndy said you'd kill me if I didn't call and tell you that I'll be going in for surgery while you're away."

"What? Uh, yeah, Dad, I would! Especially since I didn't even know. What's going on?"

"My doctor recommended it. It's to remove the diseased part of my intestine. That way I won't ever have to deal with diverticulitis while I'm off traveling." He reminded me that he had to cancel his trip to Chile earlier in the year when he went into the hospital.

"Yeah, I remember. I also remember that you were talking about doing this before Jenna's graduation." I had specifically asked him to wait until afterwards as I was intuitively feeling that something bad was going to happen to him in the hospital, and that he wouldn't make it. "I still feel really uneasy about this, Dad. Did you get a second opinion?"

"Yeah, I talked to my family doc and he estimated my need for the surgery at fifty-one percent, given that I love to travel to out-of-the-way places. He told me that if I promised only to travel to cities with topnotch medical care, like London or New York, then I shouldn't do it, but you know me."

I was stunned. "Fifty-one percent? That's not a reason to have surgery. I don't think you should do it." I tried to reason with him. "I mean, are you aware of all the complications involved? Not to mention the dangers of anesthesia. Are they saying anything about a colostomy bag? Look, you need to do what you need to do, but let me tell you every time that Ian had surgery, he'd end up with every one of the possible complications."

The worst was when the doctors wanted to take a lung biopsy because Ian had some sort of lesion that they couldn't figure out from the scans, so they told us that there was a "remote, unlikely" chance they might have to cut his rib to reach the spot that they needed the tissue from. They ended up cutting his rib, causing him long-term excruciating pain. And after all that, the results of the biopsy were inconclusive.

"I'm confident that it'll go well. The colostomy bag is really not even in the equation. They just go in, cut out the damaged intestine and then reattach it." He explained they could do it all laproscopically.

"Okay, Dad, as long as you're sure. I'm going to be really mad if something happens to you and I have to come home early!" I joked. But I was nervous and just trying to hide it.

"I'll be fine. Have a wonderful trip, and I can't wait to hear all about it."

"Thanks, Dad. I love you"

"I love you, too."

Then I hung up.

****

While being with Jenna in Europe, the whole concept of having a baby and raising her only to send her on her way at the age of eighteen seemed rather strange to me. This thought crossed my mind rather frequently. It reminded me of when Ian died, and I was shown heaven. I felt joyous for him, but it hurt that I had to stay here and figure out the next steps without him. Jenna had grown up, and I was filled with happiness that she had made it to this step, but it also meant I had to figure out how to move forward in my own life without her being part of my every day. And soon, Robbie would be off on his own too—where did the years go?

At this point Robbie was sixteen, and had lived more than half his life without Ian there to see him grow up. In eighth grade his class had to do a project on philanthropy. In honor of his dad, Robbie decided to work on Relay for Life, an American Cancer Society sponsored event. That year, he was the single largest fundraiser in our town of Ridgefield. Over the three following years, he raised more than $10,000 for this cause. He has spoken to audiences around the state where he receives standing ovations when he tells his story. He also dedicated his free time to the Appalachia Service Project, an organization that helps make homes warmer, safer and dryer in Appalachia. And he is a Boy Scout.

Certainly my kids are not perfect, as they've had their fair share of teenage angst; however as difficult as it was to lose their father at such young ages, Jenna and Robbie both turned into enormously compassionate people.

****

Jenna and I arrived home on the same day my dad got home from the hospital. He'd had surgery four days earlier, and apparently all had gone well; the doctors were pleased with his progress. As soon as I got home, I called his house in Denver. Cyndy told me he had just gotten there and was asleep on the couch. She would have him call me later that day or over the weekend.

By Sunday night, I had not heard from Dad, but I figured he would call me when he was up to it. I wanted to see how he was doing, and was eager to talk to him about his plans to help my kids financially with college. He had mentioned it in passing several times, but I was never brave enough to press him for the details; I didn't want to pester him about this while he was recovering. I was getting a bit antsy because Jenna was just three weeks from heading off to college. Still, I thought, what difference could a few more days make?

On Monday, I received a flurry of emails from Cyndy saying that Dad had experienced a lot of pain Sunday evening. She had taken him to the doctor that morning, but they couldn't find anything wrong. Because he was in so much pain, they decided to readmit him to the ICU that afternoon.

Cyndy's email message was filled with lighthearted jokes and banter, more or less making fun of my father for not being able to tolerate the pain. She explained that the doctors thought it was "battle fatigue," which is when your body suffers post-traumatic pain after surgery. I was sure the banter was Cyndy's way of dealing with the stress, but I just wanted to know what was going on without trying to read between the lines. It didn't occur to me to pick up the phone and call her. We had never been close, even though she had been in my father's life for almost twenty years. Given that Cyndy was my dad's third wife, was twenty years younger than he (and roughly only ten years older than me), and that they lived over 1,800 miles away, I had never had the opportunity to get to know her. Because of the sarcastic tone of Cyndy's emails and the fact that they indicated no real problem other than pain, I was not overly concerned.

On Tuesday morning, I received a much more dire email. My father was rushed back for additional surgery. A staple had come loose and his abdomen had filled with his stomach contents. Cyndy still wasn't sounding any alarm. She said she couldn't wait to tell him, when he woke up, that he now had a colostomy bag.

I called my brother to get his take on the situation. Eric lives in Denver, not far from the hospital. I asked him if he had gone to see him.

Eric rarely spent time with Dad even though he lived close by. Constant quips about his desire to do art as a profession drove my brother away. I remember my grandfather making similar comments. "Well, Eric, that's a nice dream," he'd say, "but you can't make a livin' out of that artsy stuff. You've got to work your way up in a respectable company like I did. You need to think about a pension and benefits."

When we were younger, my brother and I really didn't interact much. I seemed to always be acting out and trying to get attention, like sneaking out at night and smoking the occasional cigarette. Eric, on the other hand, always played the role of the goody two-shoes. It wasn't until I came home early one night from babysitting, when we were both still in high school, that I discovered him and some of his friends drinking beer. That's when our relationship suddenly got interesting. *I* now had something on *him*. Ever since then we've been pretty close and during the year prior to my father's hospitalization we had gotten much closer. Eric had introduced me to teachings about the Universal Laws, which escalated my spiritual path exponentially. This new common ground expanded our friendship and led us on a beautiful shared journey.

Eric hadn't been to visit Dad. "What can I do? He's in the hospital, so he's in good hands."

"Oh my God, Eric. What if he dies?"

"What do you mean? That's not going to happen."

"Okay, so you are telling me that you are fifteen minutes from the hospital, and you don't want to see what is going on? You don't want to ask the doctors what they are saying? Maybe there are things that they're not telling us. Maybe you can't *do* anything, but you can go and support him emotionally. Wouldn't you want him to come visit you?"

I normally wouldn't speak to anyone that way, but I felt helpless—the situation was spiraling out of control. Eric was the only person who could help me understand what was going on inside that hospital.

"Fine. I'll go down, but not because I'm worried, but because you're guilting me into it."

"Good. Let me know what's going on. I'm really worried."

About an hour later, my dad's sister called. Linda is a petite woman and gentle soul who was always there for me at critical times. In fact, she and her husband John were the first of my family to arrive the day Ian died.

"Lisa, I'm really concerned about your father. Have you talked to Cyndy?"

"No, I haven't talked to her. I've just been getting email updates. I have to say I'm not happy about how she is being so sarcastic about everything. I mean..."

"Well, what are you going to do?" she cut me off.

"What am I going to do? What do you mean? There is not a lot I *can* do from here."

"Aren't you going to go out to Denver?"

At that moment, something shifted within me. I realized that I was doing exactly what my brother was doing. I was not taking responsibility.

"Uh...yes. It's almost 8 p.m. here. I'm going to book the first flight out for tomorrow morning."

"I think that's a good idea."

I booked a one-way flight to Denver, arranged for a rental car and talked to my brother. He had visited Dad, who recognized him, but the medication was making him loopy. I was glad to hear that he was awake and talking.

That night I had a dream. It was very real and extremely detailed. My dad and I were sitting in the backseat of a car. Spacious with a blue interior, it reminded me of one of my grandparents' Buicks. My grandparents were in the front driving us to a celebration for my dad. The whole family was waiting for us. My dad looked over at me and told me he wasn't feeling well and that he wanted to lie down. He put his head on my lap, and I told him it was going to be okay. Suddenly, Cyndy showed up out of nowhere and was sitting on my lap. She told me that my dad had to put his head on *her* lap. I felt crushed by the weight of her. I awoke with a foreboding, deep in my stomach.

After landing in Denver, Eric called, insisting that he was going to pick me up at the airport. Twenty minutes later, he screeched to a stop in front of me, jumped out of the car and said, "I just got the call a few minutes ago. Get in! Dad's been taken in for another emergency surgery. He was doing okay this morning and then suddenly crashed. They had to intubate him because he stopped breathing. They have no idea what's wrong."

This is why I had to come; there was a reason that I had to be there. I started crying.

At the ICU ward, we found Cyndy sitting on a beige couch by herself, looking at her Blackberry. When she looked up to see who came in the room, I could see the shadow of fear on her face and the dark circles under her eyes. She got up to give us each a tentative hug.

The doctor walked into the waiting room in his scrubs and gave us an uncertain smile. It turned out my father's colon had died. I didn't know that a colon had a life of its own, but apparently it does. He explained that in the latest emergency surgery they had removed his entire colon and then cleaned out his stomach cavity for any remaining bacteria to prevent infection. We were told that he was out of the woods and that it would take a lot longer for recovery, but that there was a very good chance that he was on the mend. In a few days he could be moved to another floor for some additional recovery time. A huge wave of relief washed over us all.

In the ICU, the bright lights were unsettling, as were all the beeping monitors and the glass-walled cubicles where the patients were cordoned off. Cyndy held back the curtain so we could enter Dad's cubicle. He was lying immobile. His eyes were closed, and he looked abnormally still. His chest rose and fell in conjunction with the whirring breathing machine next to him. An IV pole held a mess of bags—drugs hanging and fluids dripping. There were antibiotics, potassium, painkillers, blood pressure meds, nutrients, and other liquids that were supposed to help him get better. It was overwhelming.

The nurse, a thirty-something, upbeat young woman, threw the curtain back and walked into the cramped space. She smiled and went about her work, checking his vitals and making notes in the computer chart. When Ian was sick, I saw him in countless hospital situations, but never had he looked this compromised. A breathing tube was one of the few experiences Ian didn't have, and he remained conscious until the end. Seeing my father this way was beyond comprehension. *How could this have happened?*

As hopeful as the doctor was, the reality was completely different. The rest of Wednesday, my dad continued to deteriorate. By Thursday, once again the doctor remained optimistic, but the nurses continued to shake their heads and give us looks of concern and understanding. His kidneys had failed, which meant he had to use dialysis. Overnight, however, his body rejected the dialysis process.

Early Friday morning, I had another dream. This time we were at the celebration we'd been driving to in the earlier dream. It was all of my dad's family from the past and the present—a feast and celebration of his life. I told him I loved him and that I was completely fine if he wanted to go back with Grandma and Grandpa when the party was over. He didn't know what to do. He wanted to go with them, but he felt like he had things he still wanted to do. I told him that I thought it would be best if he went. He reluctantly agreed. I woke up knowing where we were headed.

That day, I could tell that my father's spirit had left his body. Cyndy told me she too had a dream where he came to her, and she told him it was okay to go. Eric took some time with him, and said the same thing. We approached the ICU doctor to discuss taking him off life support. She looked at us like we were the devil incarnate. "Well, if it were my father, I'd do everything possible to keep him alive," she said in a huff.

"If you're telling me that you can bring my father back to the active life he had then yes, let's keep up this charade and get him well and out of here. But if you are telling me that the best you can do is get him discharged from the ICU to a long-term nursing facility, where most likely he's going to be on a breathing machine for the next six months, only to die a slow torturous death—then no, that's not what we want for him."

She looked at me and walked away.

The next morning, a new team of ICU doctors, with a new mindset, arrived on the scene. Two of them approached us in the waiting room.

"We wanted to reach out to you. We're concerned that you are hoping for a miracle that we just don't see happening. We think that out of respect for your father you should consider removing life support."

One of the most frustrating parts I experienced dealing with a sick person in the hospital is the ever-changing opinions from the experts. I feel we are taught to submissively agree to those in authority, in this case the doctors. After being told the day before that we were rushing to judgment, less than twelve hours later we were told that "out of respect" we should remove life support. Ultimately, this team was on our side, but it was hard enough to deal with the idea of losing my dad, when on top of it we originally felt no support from the staff concerning what we wanted.

We were all on the same page, and within fifteen minutes the nurses had prepared him by removing his breathing machine and the IVs. We stepped into the cubicle. Cyndy and I each held his hand, and my brother put his hand on Dad's leg. I closed my eyes and immediately connected to another reality. I asked Cyndy and Eric if they wanted me to share what I was seeing. They agreed.

"I sense him above us, smiling. He wants us to know that he loves us and that he's sorry for everything that happened. He loves you so much, Cyndy, and thanks you for taking such good care of him. And Eric, he wants you to know that he is proud of you and me too. I see a great light, and he's moving toward it. I feel him reuniting with Grandma and Grandpa. Oh, it's amazing."

Tears ran down my face, not from sadness but from experiencing a realm so filled with love that I was overwhelmed with emotion.

No matter how many issues you have with someone, death seems to melt them away. In that moment, in a strange way, I felt at total peace with my dad.

****

Two days later, we arrived at the attorney's office. Though he promised that he would change his will after my brother and I spoke to him nine months earlier, my father never did. My worse-case scenario was unfolding before my eyes. Eric and I were each given a token amount. The rest of his fortune, including my grandmother's money, all folded into a family trust that would primarily be used to take care of Cyndy for the rest of her life. Cyndy, Eric and I would all be co-trustees. I was devastated. It wasn't about the amount of money that I felt I was owed; it was the principle. I felt like my father was not claiming me as his daughter. Again, it triggered my deep wounds about being adopted. It made me feel so unwanted. He'd raised us to be fair; he was always about being fair. And here he was being so devastatingly unfair.

I felt an incomparable darkness. My mind went to places it had never gone before. I felt so violated and victimized. I felt so unloved and unwanted. I hated my father. How could this be? I was barely able to breathe. Even talking to my angels and trying to glean some sort of spiritual understanding was not helping.

I turned to the only thing I could think of for additional support, my trusted spiritual advisor. I'd been working with her for over ten years, usually for an annual birthday reading and the occasional "Help me. What should I do?" situation.

She channeled my spirit guides and told me they said that my father thought I had everything, that my life was full of abundance and that I didn't need anything.

"What I'm getting is that he is angry with his own life. He was never able to live the way he really wanted, until he was in his last career. He's just now understanding after his death that his inability to follow his passion caused great harm to you and your brother."

After hearing this, my anger was quieted. We were not that different, my father and I. We both had lived a lie. I'd hidden who I really was for years, and my father had done the same. I had just found my way to Spirit sooner.

CHAPTER 12

On a Thursday morning, three-and-a-half months after my father's death, I woke with a shot of adrenaline. Down in my bones, I was driven by an urgent need to transcribe a message; it was about my father. For all I knew, it may have been my dad who was trying to contact me. I rushed out of bed, down to my computer and started typing.

Since I started channeling, messages would normally come to me when I was awake. Information came randomly, directly through the Universe. I knew it had nothing to do with my cognitive ability; it came from a shift in consciousness. The messages that came through, whether they were for myself or someone else, were always perfect, clear and profound. However, that morning was the first and only time I was jolted out of a sound sleep by a message. This one began:

Your father now realizes that money is the blood life-force of a secondary organism, or 'body' that is part of the earth form.

I knew the message meant that we have bodies that are one entity and that money is another, separate entity. I understood it to mean that money was an energy exchange that exists as real as our flesh. The language can be strange when I channel, and I thought of this as a translation issue. Putting metaphysical truth in human terms can be complicated. When the language sounded foreign, it was confirmation to me that it was not coming from my own mind, but rather somewhere else.

In order to grow money, you need to exercise it and freely exchange it with others through commerce, building dreams and overall to strengthen the larger purpose of this entire "earth state" experiment. Money is not to be locked up and squirreled away.

This statement came through me with the force and directness of a lightning bolt. I wasn't even thinking—I was just typing. The voice seemed to transition into my father speaking.

By controlling the money, I now realize that I inhibited the spiritual growth of my children and negatively impacted the security of my wife. If I were to restructure the money that was left on earth, as it does me no good here, and after all that work (here, I heard him laugh) *I would leave the house to Cyndy. I'd evenly split the money from my parents' estate and give it to Eric and Lisa in its entirety. I would honor my intention of helping my grandchildren complete their undergraduate degrees with financial support.*

You will notice that the way I constricted my money on earth was a mirror image of what occurred in my body—be aware of what you are doing in every area of your life, as your body will be a reflection of that.

Cyndy, as much as I loved you on earth, my love for you has expanded beyond measure. I wish that I could have expressed my love more openly and freely. I now know that through conditioning, all people on earth put far too many limits on the love they express. If I'd known then what I know now, I would have been a different human being, and I would have appreciated you more.

Please know that I am sorry for any and all pain that was caused by my ignorant actions. I would have never been able to articulate this on earth, as I was so blinded by my upbringing and lack of awareness. I hope that I can do right, so that you may all have what you need and more. Life on earth is to be lived fully. I challenge each of you to dream big and then take the actions to make your dreams come true.

Please remember me for my strengths and not for my weaknesses. I am ashamed of how I was so ignorant, when the answers are so clearly all around us if we can only wake up to see them.

I finished typing and sat stunned. Even though I felt the truth of the message, I worried that the information seemed too self-serving. *Was the message real? Was it really from my father? Were my needs somehow influencing the message?*

Finally, I accepted it for truth for a simple reason: I believe in what I do. I shared it with my brother, though not with Cyndy. I felt that if she discounted the message because it was about Dad's money, it would mean she was discounting everything I do. In the end, I felt like she may have gotten the money, but I got the gift of an ongoing connection to my dad. I had planned to share with Cyndy the specific message my father had given me about her, but when I flew to Denver to attend the first trustee meeting, she explained she was too busy to meet with me before or afterwards. I took this as a sign that she wasn't ready to hear it.

As I pondered the message over the next few weeks, I realized I had always blamed my father for a lack in my life. Upon his death, I saw a new side of my father, a side he had cleverly kept hidden and secret. I saw the parts that kept him from being emotionally able to be close to others, the parts that he yearned to express as fatherly love, but was unable. He had broken bits that had shattered so deep within, he couldn't even begin to pick up the pieces and repair himself. It wasn't my father who I should blame, it was humanity itself. I blame the way we are socialized and "trained" not to follow our passions, not to speak our truth, and not to be just who we were born to be.

I also realized that my dad was exactly who he was, so I could more clearly see who I am. He and I agreed, long before we showed up on this planet, that he would play his part, and I would play mine, so we could each reflect to one another our light and our darkness – so that we could grow. If everything in our lives were rainbows and puppies, we would never evolve, and isn't that the idea? We come back, time and again, so we can explore new and different facets of ourselves. However, when we get here we forget who we really are, so it all gets rather tricky. It's only when we can connect to divine wisdom and *remember* who we are that things here on earth get just a little bit easier.

Ian's death too, I believe, was not the result of a savage seven-year battle with cancer, but actually from this conflict. For forty-four years, he fought to be who he really was born to be and it eventually became too much for him to bear. Yes, of course his physical body failed after three stem-cell transplants, countless rounds of chemotherapy, and unknown amounts of radiation particles being harpooned into his cells—but it was his soul that called it a wrap for this earthly adventure. He wasn't following his bliss, his mission or his calling in life. He was even given a wake up call, which was the gift of four years of remission after his first stem-cell transplant. Yet, he never changed his outlook on life or altered the way he was living it—his time was up.

I'd put so much energy into expecting to receive this money; finally I realized that money was all around me. Since channeling that message on that morning, I've intensively studied the universal teachings of money and life, and how to create a spiritual business using universal laws. It was my father's death, the issues surrounding his will, and his message that taught me this: We cannot latch on to a person or organization as our source of income. *The Universe* is our source. Money comes to us from the Universe through the people we serve. Understanding this has given me profound freedom.

Since that first channeling session, my deceased father has been the most active dead man I know. He's visited me, my friends and my clients regularly.

He came through as a vision to one of my clients while we were in the middle of a healing session. He showed himself to a friend of mine in her dream. She visualized my house and saw him sitting on the couch. A month later she came to my home for a dinner party and was shocked as my house was exactly what she saw in her dream—she had never been here before.

During a recent training weekend, my mentor channeled a message from my father to me. Everyone else got messages from Buddha, Jesus and other ascended masters—thanks Dad!

He contacted me twice through my former teacher and well-known medium, Roland Comtois, at two events where only a handful of people were given messages.

He came through to my brother's girlfriend in a healing session she had with a gifted energy healer.

Finally, he leaves me signs when I think about him—in the form of cigarette smoke or white butterflies.

His messages are often about how he now understands what I'm doing and that he is tremendously proud of me! Who would have thought that I would finally hear those long sought-after words from my dad *after* he died. He seems to always be hanging around wanting to be a part of the action. It's almost like he's taken the role of my behind-the-scenes business manager.

Who knows, maybe he's lining things up for me right now.

Another significant shift has happened since my father's death. I was able to put Jenna's departure to college into perspective and release all grief and anxiety around it. She is off living her life now, passionately and with love. She must be free to fly, to find her alignment with Spirit. As with all of us, such is her divine right.

As my gift continues to strengthen and be shared and spread, I can feel how my soul is singing—literally and figuratively. My physical body is finding balance and harmony, and my life continues to be filled with more blessings. I believe this is because I am following my true, divine purpose. Miracles are happening in my life each and every day that I work directly with Spirit/God/Universe. I have never felt more fulfilled in my life. And yet, the fire I've walked through for my spiritual healing has been almost unbearable. It's been arduous, nearly impossible at times. Each and every day, I wake up and say, "Yes! Thank you for my life. Please allow me to be of service. Please show me what my purpose is and how I can help more people today. Please let me be my best self today."

****

On December 14, 2012 a gunman stormed Sandy Hook Elementary School in Newtown, Connecticut, killing twenty children and six adults. This tragic event happened less than eighteen miles from my home in Ridgefield. Like a lot of people in the area, and even in the country, I felt a profound need to do something to help, though I didn't know what. Three days later I received a broadcast email from The Ridgefield Playhouse, the venue where I had first channeled on stage earlier that year. They were announcing their plans to hold a fundraising event for Newtown—with details to follow. Without hesitation I sent an email to the director of The Playhouse:

Let me know if I can help by giving a blessing, an inspirational message or prayers at this event.

The next day I received a "Thanks—but no thanks" from The Playhouse.

Then a few emails later, I received this from Laura, the graphic designer for the cover on the first meditation CD I had produced:

Hi Lisa:

I hope this finds you well. I'm sure you are feeling the effects of last Friday's horrific events along with everyone else in our area as well as the world. I am putting together a special evening to try to help heal people's hearts and souls. I, along with National Recording artist Lucinda Rowe, am reaching out to a few select musicians and I had thought of you as well.

Would you be interested in going on stage to give an inspirational talk on love, loss and moving forward and then lead the audience on a guided meditation? I know you have the power to help heal people in this very difficult time.

When I made the offer to The Playhouse, it was done with such a deep feeling of love and concern that I didn't feel rejected when they weren't interested. The Universe heard my offer and presented it to Laura.

I immediately told her that, of course, I would do anything she thought would help. Then came the task of organizing my thoughts and putting together a small program for this fragile audience of potentially a hundred or more people. It was a daunting experience, not knowing exactly who would be there. The families? Some of the surviving students? First responders? The amount of emotion in the audience would be extreme. How do I approach someone when he or she has lost a loved one? I didn't think anyone really knew the right words to say. It was so difficult to enter that conversation with even a single individual, and here I was entering an entire *community* that had lost so much. It was overwhelming; I had no idea where to begin.

Many times I sat down with the specific intention of outlining my talk—but nothing would come. I meditated on it and the same answer kept coming to me: *Be in the moment.*

As I drove to Newtown, three or four of my best stories about love, loss and moving forward came to me. It was as though my brain was waiting for that moment to release the grip on my thoughts, or was it Spirit filling me with what I needed at exactly the right time?

The event was called "Music, Light and Love" and was held at Edmond Town Hall Theatre, a colonial revival style building in Newtown, the center of government and community activity there. A crowd of about one hundred fifty people were in attendance. It was a caring, loving atmosphere. There would be two local singer-songwriters, an inspirational speaker and me.

As I waited to be introduced, I was listening closely to the performers that were on before me. When I stepped onstage I knew everything would be okay. I spoke from my heart.

"I'm your neighbor from Ridgefield." My voice cracked, tears welled in my eyes. "I want you all to know that not only do I love you, but so does the entire town of Ridgefield. I know as well, that the state of Connecticut and every other state in our nation has you in their hearts. For that matter, so does the entire world." The audience applauded.

I went on to share my story of losing my husband after a seven-year battle with cancer. I told them how I was taken to heaven just hours before he passed, to see how they were preparing for my husband's arrival. After my husband died, I told them, I found the tools to help me move forward with my life and am now living a beautiful and happy existence. In order to keep my program in the moment, I referred to a few things the other speaker said, and referenced the musicians' comments. I then led a healing guided meditation, where they were invited to go into their hearts and envision it as a garden, watering what they loved and letting the rest go.

When it was over, people in the lobby surrounded me. Many told me they had never experienced that type of meditation and that they absolutely loved it. Others told me how meaningful my message was and that what I had said was absolutely perfect. Ultimately Spirit had guided me: It was all about being in the moment.

****

I look back at the last decade, at my path from corporate to consciousness and all the lessons I've learned and continue to learn. We are so conditioned to follow the rules and be part of the mainstream, and yet I believe that's what's killing our society. I believe a lot of violence comes from people who are prevented from being who they are. Both Ian and my father died without living their truth. So have countless others.

This path has been the hardest thing I've ever done. The rational thing would have been to go and get another accounting job. However, it would have been like committing suicide for my soul to go back to the mainstream. Sharing my love, telling the truth and being a hundred percent my authentic self has set me free. It's an ongoing path of healing that will last a lifetime. When things don't go well, I don't fall as deep as I used to. Now I have a spiritual hammock in which to rest as I do my healing. And when things do go well, I'm amazed at how every detail comes together. It's got to be Spirit!

We all came to this earth to live our soul's purpose. The only way to reach happiness is to be who we are and continue to tell our truth. The bottom line is that we all have to love ourselves. We know what love is, what truth is, what is right and what is holy.

We just have to have the courage to live it.

A MESSAGE FROM THE ANGELS

As I was completing this book, I decided to channel a message so that the angels could speak directly. While sitting in my meditation room, I closed my eyes and called on all the angels, archangels, ascended masters, my ancestors, spirit guides and any other beings of love and light. I immediately felt connected.

Expecting a gentle message of guidance, I was surprised by the intensity of what came through. It was a passionate call to action. Afterwards, though, I saw that it reflected the themes of this book, the consequences of not finding and following our authentic selves.

Learn to connect to Spirit. It's worth your time; I guarantee your life will forever be happier. Prepare, ask, listen—that's all you need to do. The Art of Living Happy has never been so easy.

Love and blessings,
Lisa

"Knowing the truth can be disconcerting for those who are so ingrained with the thoughts of others. Questioning your beliefs is healthy and productive. Ninety-nine percent of what you think and feel is born out of other peoples' experiences and words that have been spoon-fed to you. The only way for you to truly know your truth is to find the time to sit quietly, ideally in nature, and connect to that small, still voice. How often do you do this? Daily? Weekly? Monthly? Sometime in the last year? Never? This is exactly our point.

"People are so busy running from the only really good information out there. You'll find yourself running, you'll find yourself avoiding, you'll find yourself not wanting to go to that place of deep feeling because you were told that having your own truth and your own desires is not okay.

"Parents, teachers and society many times have mandated what and how and who you are. Now is the time to stop. Now is the time to take control of your life. If nothing else, decide to take five minutes a day to honor yourself. Sit down and give yourself five minutes of your time to nourish your soul. If you won't, who will?

"This is your life on earth; do not come to the end of it wishing that you had done something else with your time, energy and money. It's all up to you how your life turns out. The sooner you accept this truth, the sooner you will not tolerate anyone else telling you what to do.

"Our greatest desire is for you to awaken to the life you came here to live and to fulfill your promise to your soul that you made before being born on earth. If you follow your desires, directed by Spirit, you will achieve far more greatness than you can imagine, and your soul will sing with joy and this earth may one day know peace. The sooner you wake up the better.

"In love, joy, happiness and peace, we present to you the way to be.

Love and blessings,
The Guardians"

(This is the name of the collective group that came through to me—I don't believe I've ever channeled for them before. ~Lisa)

ACKNOWLEDGMENTS

This book has been percolating in my consciousness for almost ten years. Countless numbers of people would say to me, "You should write a book!" In retrospect I now realize those words were promptings directly from Universe to me. I want to thank each of the following people for not only helping me and encouraging me on my path of writing and publishing this book, but more importantly for being a part of my everyday life and supporting me in discovering who I am and why I am here.

Family:

My children, Jenna and Robbie ~ The two best manifested miracles I've ever conjured. Thanks for agreeing to be my kids; I know our life hasn't always been easy. Robbie, you never cease to amaze me with your generosity and compassion. Jenna, your dedication of service to others and concern for their wellbeing is heartwarming. I am proud of you both, and I love you more than you can ever know!

My husband, David ~ You are my rock, my Buddha, and my greatest supporter. I love you! I especially appreciate the clarity you have in your own life and in our life together. I look forward to our upcoming adventures....

My heavenly husband, Ian Sharpe ~ Thank you for allowing me to love you from the time we met in September 1989 until death parted us in February 2004. I love your signs and your support from above; you never cease to amaze me!

My brother, Eric Klepinger ~ Obviously blood is not thicker than water. Your support of who I am and what I do has sustained me on some of my darkest days. Introducing me to the Universal Laws has rocked my world (in a good way)! I love you, Brother.

My mother, Judith Hassig ~ I thank God every day that you are my mother. You are the one person who has always believed in me since before I can remember. I am eternally grateful and appreciative of you and your love for me. I love you more!

My stepdad, Max Smith ~ Even though you weren't a part of my life until I was an adult, you've been a wonderful role model of a loving father for me. I adore and love you!

My father, Brian Klepinger ~ As difficult as it was to share our journey together, I do love and appreciate you. I'm grateful that you've expressed your support to me. It means more than I can say. Thank you.

Friends:

Caroline Allen ~ Your encouragement as my writing coach has been invaluable! This book would have never been written without your emotional, spiritual and mental support of me over the past several years.

Nancie Benson ~ The latest and greatest addition to my life! Your insights and advice regarding my business have been invaluable. I am equally thrilled to call you a dear friend. Thank God for speed dial.

Lee Casey ~ I'm so glad we met during my short real estate career. Your ideas helped open my mind and my heart. Thank you for being a big part of my early awakening.

Wendy Curran ~ Thank you for helping me finish the book with your stunning copy editing skills. You are a blessing.

Pattie Holzhauer ~ I so appreciate your friendship. I love how much fun we have, like going to the Cannes Film Festival. You've always been there for me when I needed a shoulder to cry on, especially after Ian's death.

Lisa Jacoby ~ Thank you for encouraging me to use my gifts, as well as for your extraordinary support on my path by coordinating my first group events.

Basil Jones ~ Stumbling into your yoga studio was a huge turning point for me. I now have to write another whole book about how yoga can and will transform your life.

Damon Lacey ~ The angels told me to call you, and now I know why. The logo and branding you created for me is pure magic.

Jenna Palacio ~ Thank you for bringing me peace, always.

Jon Sternfeld ~ Thank you for all your help on my book. You showed up at exactly the right time in my life. You're a real-life angel.

Rob Young ~ You were obviously a brother of mine in a past life. Since our first meeting, I knew that not only would we be friends, but co-creators in business. Thanks for being the leader of Team Happy!

Mentors:

I have studied with the following people and want to express my gratitude for their wisdom and knowledge: Achito, Karen Rauch Carter, Mishi & Tim Clauberg, Roland Comtois, Marge Courtney, Raffaello Di Meglio, Wayne Dyer, Trudy Griswold, Kathryn Harwig, John Holland, Dona Ho Lightsey, Anna Linley, Denise Linn, Amy Mims, David Neagle, Cheryl Richardson, Don E. Smith, Reid Tracy and Stephanie Bennett Vogt.

To my clients and audience members who believe in what I do, thank you for allowing me to share my divine purpose.

A special thank you to all the people mentioned in my book. You have helped me become the person that I am.

RESOURCES

Below is a list of my all-time favorite resources for both my personal and professional life. I strongly urge you to check them out. Since my list continues to grow, be sure to go to my website for the latest and greatest information.
www.artoflivinghappy.com

MY TOP FOUR LIFE-CHANGING BOOKS
(in the order I read them)

Mind Over Back Pain, **by Dr. John Sarno**
This was the first book I read that woke me up to the connection between mind and body. I overcame six years of severe discomfort and impending surgery by implementing Dr. Sarno's suggestions. I have recommended this book to everyone that I know who has experienced back pain.

Dr. Sarno has impeccable credentials (Professor of Clinical Rehabilitation Medicine, New York University School of Medicine, and Attending Physician at the Howard A. Rusk Institute of Rehabilitation Medicine, New York University Medical Center). This book was my first step on my spiritual journey....

Dr. Robert Anthony's Advanced Formula For Total Success, **by Robert Anthony**

This book opened my mind to the idea that we have total control over what happens to us (not just between our mind and body, but what we think and what happens to us in our life). It's out of print and not well-organized, but the concepts are similar to *The Secret*. My copy is highlighted, underlined and well-worn.

Angelspeake: How to Talk With Your Angels, **by Barbara Mark and Trudy Griswold**

I purchased this after receiving my first angel reading. It explains how to connect directly to your angels. It's the first book I read that enabled me to become an active participant with Spirit as opposed to a passive recipient.

Move Your Stuff, Change Your Life: How to Use Feng Shui to Get Love, Money, Respect, and Happiness, **by Karen Rauch Carter**

I was introduced to feng shui and this book at a class I attended at Gilda's House, a cancer-support center, while Ian was undergoing cancer treatments in Seattle. As soon as I purchased this book and began implementing some of its ideas into our hotel room, many positive events began to unfold. This book is easy and fun to read and will work miracles in your life. I also highly recommend working with her personally or even becoming one of her certified practitioners.

MY OTHER FAVORITE BOOKS
(in alphabetical order by title)

Animal-Speak: The Spiritual & Magical Powers of Creatures Great & Small, by Ted Andrews

Archangels & Ascended Masters: A Guide to Working and Healing with Divinities and Deities, by Doreen Virtue, Ph.D.

Ask and It Is Given: Learning to Manifest Your Desires, by Esther & Jerry Hicks

Diary of a Psychic: Shattering the Myths, by Sonia Choquette

Eat, Pray, Love: One Woman's Search for Everything Across Italy, India and Indonesia, by Elizabeth Gilbert

The Four Agreements: A Practical Guide to Personal Freedom, by Don Miguel Ruiz

Healing with the Angels, by Doreen Virtue, Ph.D.

How to Rule the World from Your Couch, by Laura Day

The Intuitive Advantage, by Kathryn Harwig

The Little Soul and the Sun, by Neale Donald Walsch

Many Lives, Many Masters, by Brian L. Weiss

A New Earth: Awakening to Your Life's Purpose, by Eckhart Tolle

Sacred Space: Clearing and Enhancing the Energy of Your Home, by Denise Linn

The Seat of the Soul, by Gary Zukav

The Seven Sacred Flames, by Aurelia Louise Jones

Trust Your Vibes: Secret Tools for Six-Sensory Living, by Sonia Choquette

The Untethered Soul: The Journey Beyond Yourself, by Michael Singer

Waking Moments: A Guide to Everyday Spiritual Experiences, by Matthew Kay and Bruce Zboray

You Are a Badass: How to Stop Doubting Your Greatness and Start Living an Awesome Life, by Jen Sincero

You Can Heal Your Life, by Louise L. Hay

Your Spacious Self: Clear Your Clutter and Discover Who You Are, by Stephanie Bennett Vogt

SERVICES

Andrew French, a photographer and filmmaker in NYC. You can reach him at afrench@bway.net or by calling 917-945-2280. I saw his work in a magazine and tracked him down so he could shoot my publicity photos. I love his genius using natural light.

Art of Storytelling, a coaching service for writers, www.artofstorytellingonline.com. Caroline Allen coached me on the writing of this book. If you have a dream of writing a book, this is who you want guiding you on your journey. Her brilliance is unparalleled.

Basil Yoga, a soul-nurturing yoga studio, in North Salem, New York. www.basilyoga.com. Basil Jones is my yoga guru and I love the yoga kula (community) that has been created here.

Bloom Your Dreams, a coaching service helping people achieve significant levels of success that is their divine birthright, www.cherylbartlett.com. Every time I talk to Cheryl Bartlett, she shares a mind-blowing new tool with me. Working with her has been life-changing.

EJK Art, Eric Klepinger is a fine artist who focuses on capturing the spirit that is within all things. He uses his artistic perspective to help clients realize their own creative potential with whole brain exercises, whether they work in the corporate world or as artists. You can learn more at www.EJKArt.com.

Lacey Creative, a high-end graphic design/creative service specializing in custom logo design and eye-catching brand identity, www.laceycreative.com. Damon Lacey helped me stand out when he created my remarkable logo as well as this book cover. He has fun and original ideas that work.

Nancie Benson, Intuitive Business Strategy. Nancie Benson provides guidance and intuitive strategies to help business owners turn their passions and gifts into a business and lifestyle they love. She has the unique ability to intertwine her intuitive knowledge with your desired outcome, www.NancieBenson.com. She has personally given me some of the best advice I have ever received.

Positive Reflections, a service that provides fashion, wardrobe and image consulting, www.posreflections.com. Pam Friedlander helped me overhaul my closet and create my ideal style. One of the best investments I've ever made.

Social Results Today, social media management with a conscience, www.socialresultstoday.com. If you are in the consciousness field, Rob Young is the man to manage your social media—there is no one better.

The Speech Wiz, a service that helps speakers find their voice of authentic authority, www.donesmith.com. Don E. Smith is passionate about speaking and is filled with awe-inspiring stories. He coached me for my first on-stage speaking event and can take your speech to the next level.

OTHER RECOMMENDATIONS

Essential Being Meditations, by Lisa Jones. Check out my first CD—it's a great way to start a meditation practice or help you gain consistency on a daily basis. Each meditation is five minutes long. Purchase this on Amazon.com.

Soul Coaching® Oracle Cards: What Your Soul Wants You to Know, by Denise Linn. My favorite oracle cards; which are easy to use and have upbeat and positive guidance. You can also buy these on Amazon.com.

Super Soul Sunday, a television series on the OWN network where Oprah interviews today's spiritual leaders, www.oprah.com/own. I receive a lot of inspiration from this show and love that Oprah is showcasing these amazing people.

ABOUT THE AUTHOR

LISA JONES is known for her authentic ability to connect to Spirit on a compassionate level. As an inspirational speaker, radio and TV personality, workshop leader, and through her social media following, she inspires thousands around the world. Connecting people to Spirit is her life's passion.

A cum laude graduate of the University of Denver, she has a degree in accounting and a minor in international studies. She received her Certified Public Accountant designation (and is a proud member of the 300 Club) in 1989 while working in the tax department at Price Waterhouse in San Francisco. She also worked in the Environmental Consulting Practice at Ernst & Young while living in Washington D.C. Later, she became a stay-at-home mom and caregiver to her dying husband, which led her to her spiritual awakening.

Under the guidance of Denise Linn in 2008, she became a certified soul coach. In 2011, she completed the Hawaiian Shamanic Light of Aloha Mystery School. Most recently, she was ordained by The Sanctuary of the Beloved & The Order of Melchizedek, and became certified in Violet Alchemy® Dowsing after a nine-month course of study. She resides with her family in Connecticut.

Website: www.artoflivinghappy.com
Facebook: www.facebook.com/ArtOfLivingHappy
Twitter: twitter.com/LisaLivingHappy

LISA JONES is available for keynotes, lectures and workshops. To inquire about a possible public speaking appearance, please contact info@artoflivinghappy.com.